Bushwalks
IN THE SOUTH-WEST

DEPARTMENT OF CONSERVATION AND LAND MANAGEMENT

Published by: Dr Syd Shea, Executive Director, Department of Conservation and Land Management, 50 Hayman Road, Como, Western Australia 6152.
Managing Editor: Ron Kawalilak.
Editor and Compiler: Carolyn Thomson.
Features: Carolyn Thomson.
Design and Production: Tiffany Aberin.
Front Cover: Mount Frankland National Park. Photo - Dennis Sarson/Lochman Transparencies.
Back Cover: Tassel bush and tingle bark, Ancient Empire Trail. Photo - Michael James/CALM.
Maps*: Louise Burch.
Illustrations: Gooitzen van der Meer, Ian Dickinson.

*The mud maps and text are based on information supplied by CALM staff.

Acknowledgements:
Rod Annear, Carl Beck, Jesse Brampton, Lola Broadhurst, Verna Costello, Peter Dans, Steve Dutton, Anna Gemer, Kelly Gillen, Brenda Hammersley, Peter Henderson, Ian Herford, Graham Hick, Annie Keating, Jesse MacIver, Peter Morris, Tammie Reid, Allan Rose, Charlie Salaman, Neil Taylor, Klaus Tiedemann, John Watson, Glenn Wilmott, Cliff Winfield, Kim Williams, Mitzi Vance and Jennifer Young.
St John Ambulance for First Aid Information.
Bob Cooper for Outdoor Safety Information.

A special thank you to CALM's South Coast, Southern Forest and Central Forest and Swan regions; the Department's Bibbulmun Track Project; the Shire of Busselton; the Greenbushes Eco-cultural Discovery Centre; and Denmark Tourist Bureau.

ISBN 0 7309 6862 6

FOREWORD

Welcome to *Bushwalks in the South-West*, the third book in our popular series. Its follows on from the highly successful *Family Walks in Perth Outdoors* and *More Family Walks in Perth Outdoors*.

The walks are ideal for families and most of them can be completed in a couple of hours. They are intended to provide interest, variety and exercise, while encouraging WA's residents and visitors alike to enjoy the State's wonderful natural assets.

This book complements *Wild Places, Quiet Places*, CALM's guide to natural recreation areas in the South-West, and, like that popular publication, it is aimed at helping and encouraging WA's residents and visitors alike to enjoy the State's wonderful natural assets.

EXECUTIVE DIRECTOR
Department of Conservation and Land Management

CONTENTS

INTRODUCTION

THE JARRAH FOREST

THE LIMESTONE COAST

THE KARRI FOREST

MOUNTAINS AND SEA CLIFFS

THE VAST SOUTH-EAST

INTRODUCTION

ABOUT THIS BOOK

Bushwalks in the South-West is designed to extend CALM's best selling books *Family Walks in Perth Outdoors* and *More Family Walks in Perth Outdoors* outside the Perth metropolitan area.

The 40 walks described in this book are grouped into regions (The Jarrah Forest; The Limestone Coast; The Karri Forest; Mountains and Sea Cliffs; and The Vast South-East) that correspond to those in CALM's popular recreation guide to the South-West, *Wild Places, Quiet Places*. Each walk is also numbered and these numbers are used in the contents page. There is also an index by walk length on page 163.

Each walk has a mud map and a description of some of the things you may see along the way. The majority of walks have car parks and picnic facilities at the start or nearby. Some have toilets, water or other facilities.

Distances and travelling times are approximate and walk times are based on taking a leisurely stroll rather than a brisk walk.

The walk grades are given only as a guide to how difficult or strenuous each walk might be and do not reflect how safe it is. They are as follows:

- Grade 1 - Short, easy walks suitable for people of all ages and fitness levels.
- Grade 2 - As Grade 1, but longer than about three kilometres.
- Grade 3 - Suitable for people with a moderate level of fitness and will generally be longer than about three kilometres.
- Grade 4 - As Grade 3, but will have steps or short uneven stretches that may be loose or slippery underfoot.
- Grade 5 - Long or strenuous walks for experienced or fit walkers. Trails may be unmarked and go over steep, slippery or uneven surfaces.

While every effort is made to ensure that the information provided in this book is accurate, no responsibility can be taken for changes made since the walks were surveyed, or for the state of repair of any walk, as this is subject to weather or usage. When walking in the bush or along established trails, it is important to tread carefully and keep an eye open for potential hazards.

Your safety is our concern, but your responsibility.

WALKING IN THE SOUTH-WEST

The natural environment of the South-West can be divided into five natural communities or ecosystems characterised by the soil type, landform and dominant plant life:

- the jarrah forest from the Darling Range to Manjimup;
- the limestone coast between Mandurah and Augusta;
- the karri forest from Manjimup to Walpole;
- the mountains and sea cliffs of the South Coast;
- the scenically grand coastline of the Esperance area.

The Jarrah Forest from the Darling Range to Manjimup

Jarrah trees dominate the forest. Marri is the second most common forest tree, and grows intermixed with jarrah. Blackbutt is frequently found in moist, fertile valleys. Common plants of the understorey include bull banksia, blackboys, zamia palms and wattles. Wildflowers vary according to the type of soil, but the purple pea-shaped flower of the hovea is found throughout the forest during early spring. The brilliant red and golds of the flame pea, yellow hibbertias, blue leschenaultias and a range of orchids can also be seen.

The Limestone Coast between Mandurah and Augusta

The limestone coast between Mandurah and Busselton is dominated by stately tuart trees, with their lush understorey of peppermints. The rugged coast that runs between Cape Naturaliste and Cape Leeuwin has long been a popular holiday destination. Leeuwin-Naturaliste National Park, running along this coast from Bunker Bay to Augusta, protects around 15 500 hectares of rocky coastline, caves, coastal heathlands, jarrah, banksia and melaleuca woodlands and swamps.

The Karri Forest from Manjimup to Walpole

Towering, pale-skinned karri trees, which rise to heights of 85 metres, gnarled marris and, further south, tingle trees dominate the landscape between Manjimup and Walpole, deep in the cool, well-watered South-West. Cool rivers flow among the giant trees, and on the coast forest streams give way to wide river mouths and windswept heathlands. In spring, between September and November, the forest wildflowers are at their best.

The Mountains and Sea Cliffs of the South Coast

Rugged granite headlands, windswept heathland, sheltered bays and spectacular coastal scenery characterise the national parks and reserves of the Albany coast. The coastal heaths are rich in colourful wildflowers, many of them unique to the area. Inland, the peaks of the Stirling and Porongurup ranges stand in sharp contrast to the surrounding flat agricultural land. They protect a great variety of wildlife, vegetation and scenery.

The Vast South-East

Distances are greater, towns fewer and the parks and reserves much more remote, in the Esperance region, from Bremer Bay to Israelite Bay. Much of the farmland was only cleared in the 1950s or later, and the reserves here often protect near-pristine native environments. The fragile vegetation communities of WA's southern coast contain an enormous variety of flowering plants, many of which are found only here and nowhere else in the world.

WALKING SAFELY

There are basically two forms of walking in the South-West: strolling along an existing walktrail in a park, reserve, forest or bushland area or along a river bank, or trekking through wild bush elsewhere. This book deals primarily with the first.

However, all natural areas have a degree of danger; for example, slippery or uneven surfaces. Walking along tracks, trails and firebreaks is relatively safe, but you should still be alert to potential hazards. Watch for the following signs when you are walking, and take the special precautions they advise. Walks considered to be particular risk areas are also marked in this book.

Mountain Risk Area. You need to be fit and agile, be prepared to scramble up steep rock sections and encounter loose and slippery rock. Sturdy footwear is essential.

Tree Risk Area. Branches may fall from trees at any time, even healthy trees. Strong winds increase the danger of falling limbs. Creaking noises may serve as a warning.

Coast Risk Area. Keep well clear of the sea. Watch for freak waves and swells. Be wary of strong winds and slippery rocks. Stay on the path. Do not explore alone.

Rock Risk Area. Uneven and slippery rocks. Stay on defined walktrails. Stand well back from the water's edge. Never walk on wet or mossy rocks.

Cliff Risk Area. Beware of high cliffs, undercut cliff edges, loose rocks and unstable surfaces. Stay well back from the cliff edge.

Poison Risk Area. Poison baits have been placed in this area to protect native wildlife from feral animals. 1080 poison is lethal to domestic dogs and cats. Never bring your pets into baited areas.

Mosquito Risk Area. Mosquitoes in this area can carry Ross River Virus, especially during spring and early summer. Reduce mosquito bites by covering up with loose clothing and using mosquito repellent. Camp in mosquito-proof tents or use bed nets.

Be prepared

- Wear sturdy but comfortable footwear. Training shoes may be suitable, but care should be taken when crossing uneven or slippery surfaces like mossy rocks. In these cases, it is desirable to wear boots that give some support to the ankles. Always wear good quality, fairly thick, cotton or wool socks.
- Long socks or long trousers will protect legs against prickly vegetation or biting insects. A long-sleeved shirt will help to protect you from sunburn in summer and a woollen sweater or fleecy sweatshirt will help to keep you warm in winter. It is best to dress in layers of light clothing.
- Take a light raincoat, and wear a hat for protection against the sun or rain.
- Use sunscreen with a minimum sun protection factor (SPF) of 15+.
- Carry gear in a light haversack or shoulder bag, so your hands are free.
- If you are making an extended or difficult walk, tell at least two people and advise them when you've completed it.
- Take a first aid kit and insect repellent.
- Tell someone where you are going and how long you expect to be away.
- Walk in a party of two or more. If you are injured, you will need someone who can summon help.
- Make sure you have at least one litre of water per person on most days, and at least two litres on hot days.

If you become lost:

- Try to retrace your steps until you reach a recognisable place on the map.
- If you cannot retrace your steps, follow a track; it will usually lead to some habitation. Alternatively, head for the nearest high point and climb to the summit. You will then be able to see roads and areas of habitation.
- If you are still lost and have run out of water, remember that animal trails always lead to water. Watch out for flocks of birds; they fly rapidly towards water and more slowly when travelling away from water after drinking.

First Aid

Carry a first aid kit with the following basic essentials:

- Antiseptic cream and swabs
- Aspirin and Paracetamol
- Band aids
- Butterfly wound enclosures
- Dressings (sterile)
- Scissors
- Snake bite bandage
- Triangular bandage
- Tweezers

Snake bites

It is very unlikely that you will see a snake, let alone be bitten by one. Snakes sense the vibration of approaching footsteps and tend to flee into the undergrowth. If you are unlucky enough to be bitten, assume the snake is poisonous and take the following action:

DO NOT panic: Try to remain calm, lie down and immobilise the bitten area.
DO NOT wash the wound: Venom left on the skin will help doctors to identify the snake and administer the appropriate tourniquet.
DO NOT apply a tourniquet: Take out the snake bandage and bind, not too tightly, along the limb, starting at the bite area, then bandage down the limb and continue back up above the bite area. This will help to prevent the spread of the venom through the body. Do not remove the bandage.
DO NOT elevate the limb or attempt to walk or run: Movement will encourage the spread of the venom through the body. If necessary, immobilise the limb with a splint. Lie down and keep still until help arrives.
DO NOT attempt to catch the snake: Two bitten people will be more difficult to deal with than one, and if there are only two of you, you'll need someone who can go for help.

Sprains and broken limbs

Although most walks in this book are along existing well-used trails, some have uneven or loose surfaces along the route. Where possible, these have been indicated in the text, but you should always tread carefully as areas can become loose or uneven after heavy rain or very dry periods. If you or a fellow walker trips and sprains or breaks a limb, apply the 'RICE' technique:

R - REST and reassure the casualty.
I - ICE: Apply an ice pack, or cloth soaked in cold water, for 20 minutes. It may be reapplied every two hours for the first 24 hours.
C - COMPRESSION: Bandage the sprain firmly.
E - ELEVATE the sprained limb and support the injury.

Remember to avoid both heat and massage.

If the limb is broken and the casualty is conscious and breathing freely:
DO control any bleeding.
DO rest and reassure the casualty.
DO immobilise the fractured limb with splints and slings in the most comfortable position and check the blood circulation past the last bandaging point. Be sure to handle the casualty carefully.
DO NOT pull on any fractures.
DO NOT give the casualty anything to drink.
DO NOT force or straighten fractured joints.

The First Aid information provided here is very basic. St John Ambulance Australia publishes First Aid manuals and runs a variety of First Aid courses. For more information contact your nearest St John Ambulance Centre.

WHAT YOU NEED TO KNOW

Bushwalking

You can bushwalk in two ways: by using walktrails or trekking through wild bush. While the first is usually safe and relaxing, the second can do environmental damage and put your life at risk.

The walks in this book follow either formalised paths with signs and occasionally surfaced tracks, or well used and informally established tracks through bushland, parks or riverside areas. Some of the walks cross or form part of the Bibbulmun Track. This is a 950 kilometre long-distance walk from Kalamunda, in the Darling Range east of Perth, to Albany on the South Coast (see page 29).

Camping

While out walking you may see possible sites for a future camping expedition. In order to protect our environment, visitors may only camp at designated camping sites - usually marked with a sign in national parks, State forest or bushland areas. Please leave no rubbish or other traces of your visit. Camping fees are charged in some areas and the funds raised help to pay for the facilities and services provided.

Dieback

Some areas of forest and woodland have been infected by a soil-borne fungus (*Phytophthora cinnamomi*) that attacks the root systems of trees, shrubs and wildflowers. The disease is known to attack at least 900 plant species and many, such as banksias and dryandras, die very quickly. The fungus travels over and through the soil in water, attaching spores to roots. The rot sets in immediately.

The fungus is carried in soil or mud that sticks to boots and shoes, and the wheels, mudguards and underbodies of vehicles. When the soil or mud drops off, the fungus immediately contaminates the new area and multiplies. There is, as yet, no known cure.

Some areas in national parks and State forest are closed to vehicles to prevent dieback being carried into or spread through them. These areas are largely uninfected. You may enter on foot but you must not take vehicles, motorbikes, horses or any form of wheeled transport into these areas. When walking through infected areas, help to stop the rot by not straying from the track. Observe the signs and give our plants a chance.

Entry fees ($)

Entry fees are charged to some parks and reserves. Where a charge is made, it is indicated in this book by the symbol ($). The funds raised help to pay for the facilities and services provided.

Fire

Bushfires are a real danger, particularly during the dry summer months.

- Always use the fireplaces provided. Better still, bring your own portable stove.
- Open fires are not permitted in national parks.
- Build a stone ring in State forest if no fireplace exists, or dig a shallow pit to contain the embers.
- Clear all leaf litter, dead branches and anything else that may burn from an area of at least three metres around and above the fire. This also applies to portable stoves.
- Never leave a fire unattended.
- Make sure the fire is completely out before leaving. Use soil and water to extinguish the embers, and bury the ashes.

On certain days during the year the fire forecast is 'very high' or 'extreme'. A total fire ban exists on these days and some footpaths or whole reserves may be closed as a safety precaution. Local radio stations broadcast fire risk warnings, but please check with Shire authorities, the tourist bureau, or the nearest CALM office for advice on the fire situation.

Fishing

Fisheries regulations apply in all areas, but you should also check with the ranger in any national park. Trout and redfin perch have been stocked in some inland waters. Marron fishing is a seasonal activity by permit only. We'd like you, and others, to come back for more fishing, so help conserve fish numbers by taking only enough for your immediate needs.

Native plants and animals

In order to protect the environment, please do not disturb any native animals, and do not pick the wildflowers. Rocks, vegetation or old logs should not be removed, as these are often the homes of small creatures that depend on such habitats for existence.

Pets, Western Shield *and 1080 Baiting*

Pets are not permitted in national parks, nature reserves and water catchments. Many other shire-controlled parks and reserves have similar restrictions. If you are not sure whether dogs and/or other pets are permitted at the place you intend to visit, please leave them at home.

The Department of Conservation and Land Management is currently undertaking *Western Shield*, the world's biggest campaign against feral predators. Foxes and cats have already contributed to the extinction of 10 native mammal species, with dozens more species fighting for survival. *Western Shield* aims to reduce feral cat and fox populations through baiting programs using 1080 poison. This is the manufactured version of a poison that occurs naturally in WA and it does not harm native wildlife.

However, dogs and cats are very susceptible to 1080 poisoning, for which there is no antidote. Warning signs are placed prominently around baited areas, so visitors know there are baits around. Domestic dogs and cats should not be allowed to roam in areas that have been baited.

Rubbish

Place all litter in bins provided. If there are no bins, take your litter home with you. When camping or walking in the bush, bury organic waste at least 15 centimetres deep and at least 100 metres from any waterway, picnic area or campsite.

Vehicles

Normal road rules apply in all recreation and conservation areas. To protect wildlife habitat and the environment from erosion and dieback disease, please keep to formed roads and designated tracks at all times. Be sure to lock your vehicle if it is left unattended.

Water

Most creeks and rivers in Western Australia are dry during summer months. When you are out and about, take your own drinking water. If you do have to use water from the few permanent water points, it should be boiled before use, or purified using a commercially available purification product.

- **Be careful:** Stay on paths and help to prevent erosion. Your safety in natural areas is our concern, but your responsibility.
- **Be clean**: Take your rubbish out with you. Don't use soap or detergent in rivers or streams. They kill aquatic life.
- **Be cool**: Light fires only in fireplaces. Bring your own portable gas stove. Take notice of all fire weather forecasts.
- **Protect animals and plants**: No firearms please. Pets are not permitted in national parks and in some other areas. Check before you bring your dog or cat.
- **Stay on the road**: Follow signs and stay on the roads designated. Normal road rules apply.

The Jarrah Forest Walks 1 - 6

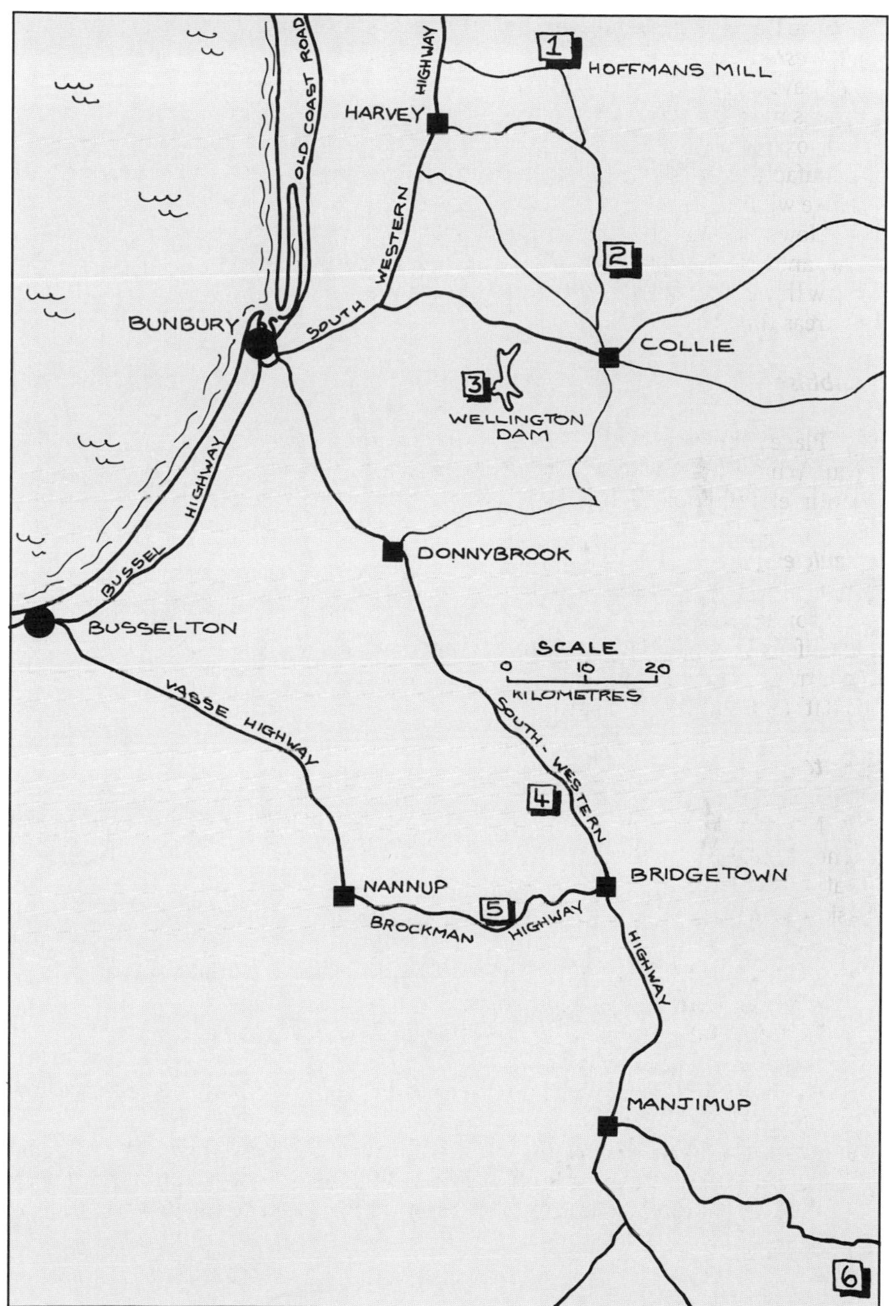

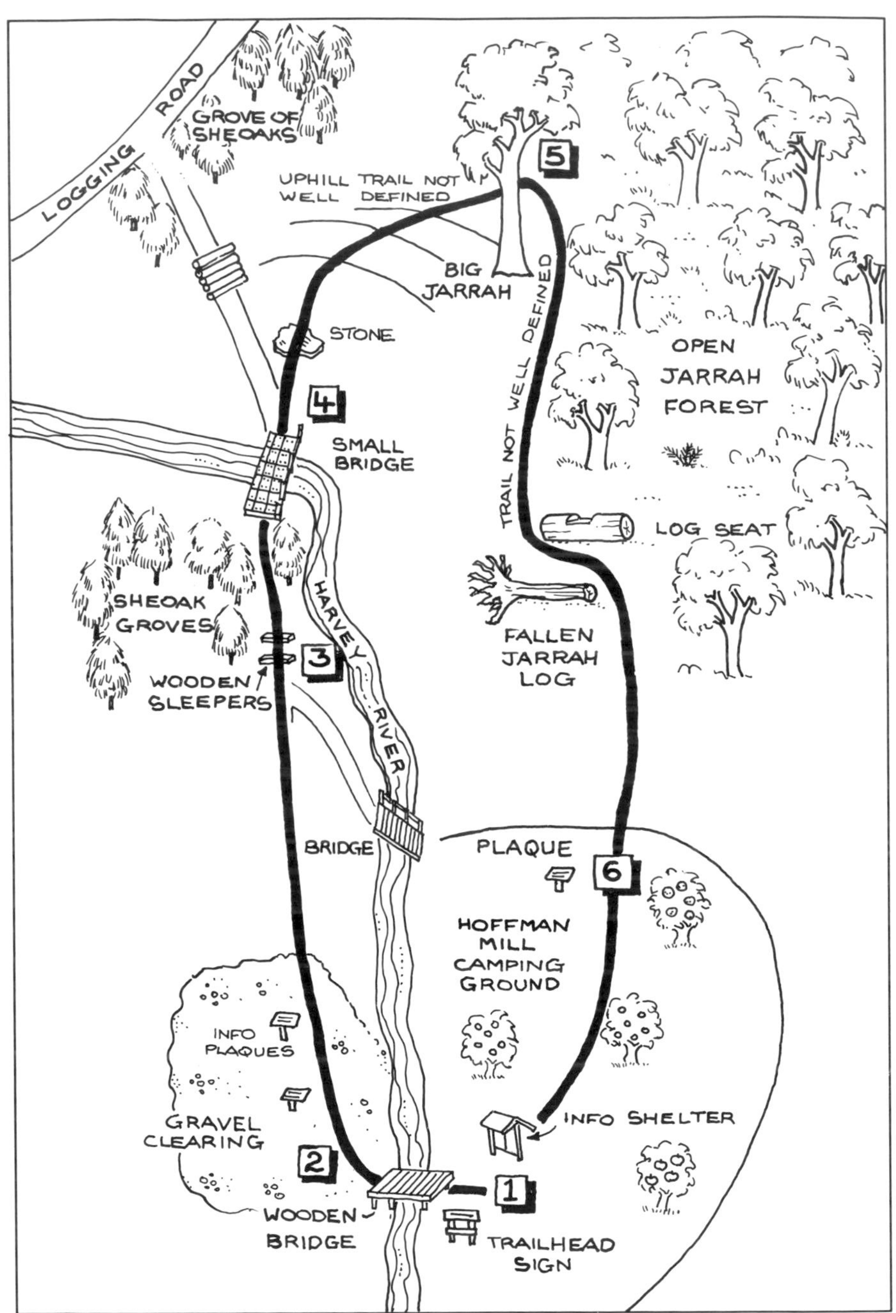
LOGGING ROAD
GROVE OF SHEOAKS
UPHILL TRAIL NOT WELL DEFINED
5
BIG JARRAH
STONE
4
SMALL BRIDGE
TRAIL NOT WELL DEFINED
OPEN JARRAH FOREST
LOG SEAT
SHEOAK GROVES
HARVEY RIVER
FALLEN JARRAH LOG
3
WOODEN SLEEPERS
BRIDGE
PLAQUE
6
HOFFMAN MILL CAMPING GROUND
INFO PLAQUES
GRAVEL CLEARING
INFO SHELTER
2
1
WOODEN BRIDGE
TRAILHEAD SIGN

Bridges Walk

1

Hoffman Mill, Harvey

***Length:** 3 km.*
***Grade:** 1.*
***Walk time:** 1 hour.*

The Bridges Walk begins at Hoffman Mill camping ground, near Harvey. You will first have to travel about 11 kilometres along a gravel road to get there. It is a scenic walk which takes you over the Harvey River and through jarrah forest. Blue markers indicate the route.

1. Begin at the trailhead sign, a short distance from the information shelter. Cross a wooden bridge over the Harvey River, where you will notice the rambling, thorny branches of blackberry. This introduced species is almost impossible to eliminate and has become a great problem along streams and rivers in the South-West, where it has taken over much of the native vegetation.
2. Just over the bridge is a gravel clearing, with parts of the old rail formation used to transport timber to the mill. The walktrail continues to the right, and two information plaques that relate to the former railway - *Sculptures of Mishap* and *Reclaiming the Line* - can be read.
3. Continue past a turn-off that heads back to the main camping ground. You should be able to see various species of hakea in the undergrowth and numerous pockets of sheoak (*Allocasuarina* species). In botanical terms, the needle-like 'leaves' of sheoak are actually branchlets. The real leaves, which encircle the joints in the needles, are so minute that they are only evident on close inspection. Wooden railway sleepers are embedded in some places along this section of trail.
4. The trail is aligned with the river for a short distance and then crosses it by means of a small wooden bridge. Not long after the bridge crossing, the trail branches. Take the right hand branch, on which a large stone creates a small step, and follow the trail uphill. Look for the blue markers to confirm you are on the right track.
5. Just after reaching a large jarrah tree (the species can be recognised by its bark, which has vertical grooves), the trail, which is now less obvious, again branches but blue markers again indicate the route. You are now in quite open forest, with a much lower and sparser understorey. The overstorey is mostly jarrah. Skirt around a fallen jarrah log to your right, admiring its gnarled roots, and another log with a seat cut in it to your left.

6. You are soon back at the camping ground. Traces of the old town can be seen in the exotic flowers and fruit trees left from the old gardens. An information plaque advises that two mills were built on this site. The first, operating between 1919 and 1930, was destroyed by fire. The second, built in 1924, was the first mill in WA to use a horizontal band saw to break down the logs. There are now several small stands of smooth-barked eastern states gum trees on the site of the old mill. These are trial plots used to test various species for their suitability in WA conditions.

Where is it? *The turn-off is along the South Western Highway, between Yarloop and Harvey. Take the Logue Brook Dam Road, and then Clarke Road. Hoffmans Mill is 18 km from the highway.*
Travelling time: *30 minutes from Yarloop or Harvey.*
Facilities: *Camping area, barbecues, tables and toilets.*
Best season: *Spring, when magnificent wildflowers are in bloom, but it is lovely all year.*

Carolyn Thomson and Mitzi Vance

JARRAH

Jarrah (*Eucalyptus marginata*) is one of the commonest and most well-known trees of the South-West. For many years it has been the principal hardwood tree harvested for timber. Its richly coloured and beautifully grained timber is sought after for cabinet making, flooring and panelling and is noted for its resistance to termites. Before the era of bitumen roads, famous roads in cities such as London and Berlin were paved with blocks of jarrah, which was called Swan River mahogany.

This stately tree has a straight trunk and grows up to 40 metres high. It sheds its rough, greyish-brown bark in long flat strips. The fibrous bark also has deep, vertical grooves. White flowers can be seen in spring and early summer. The fruits are more or less spherical to barrel-shaped, nine to 16 millimetres long and divided internally into three compartments.

Jarrah usually forms forest or woodland on gravelly soils, but sometimes also on sand or loam. It extends from Perth to Albany, with outlying populations as far north as Mt Lesueur and as far inland as Jilakin Rock.

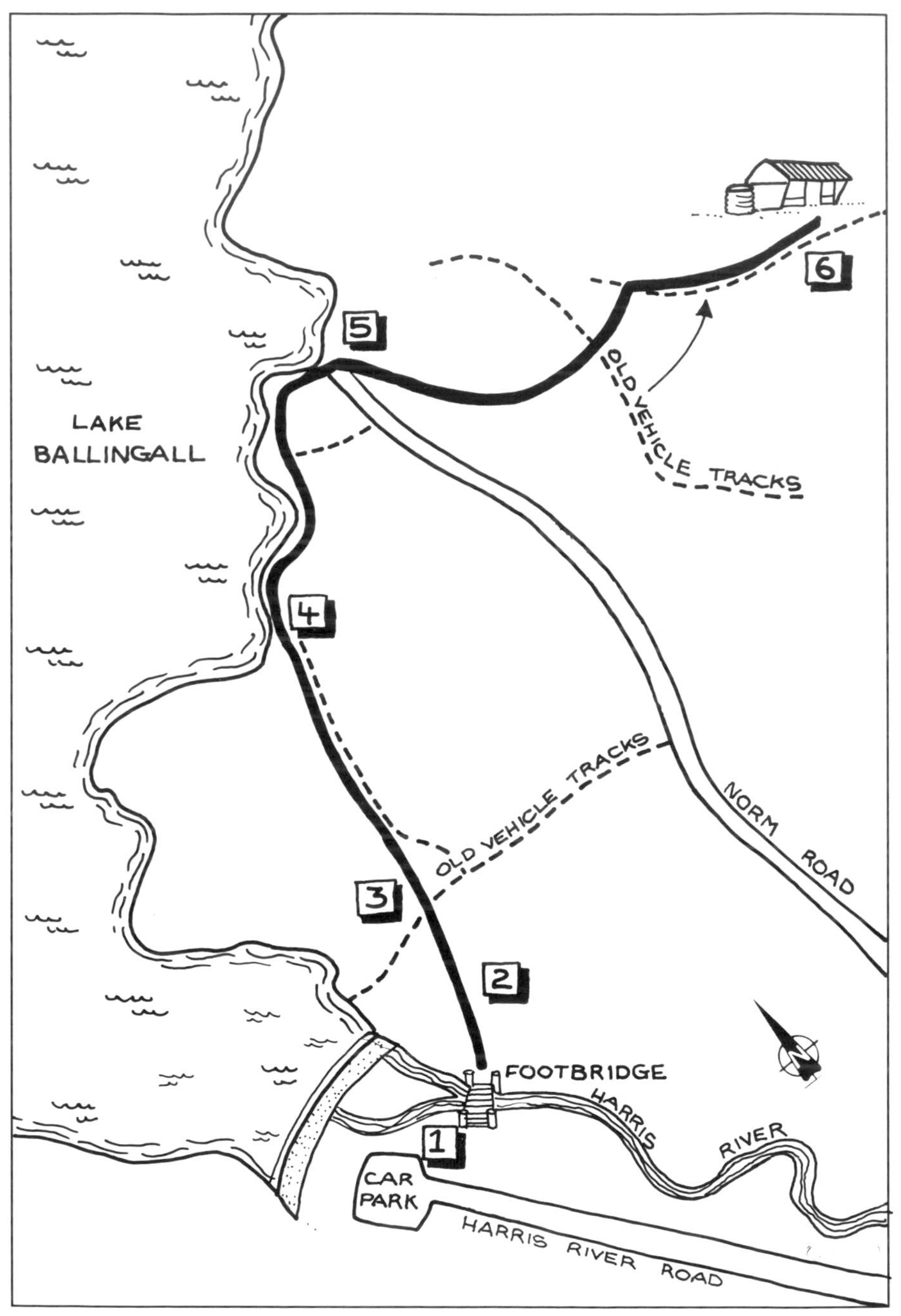
LAKE
BALLINGALL
5
6
OLD VEHICLE TRACKS
4
OLD VEHICLE TRACKS
NORM ROAD
3
2
FOOTBRIDGE
HARRIS
RIVER
1
CAR PARK
HARRIS RIVER ROAD

Harris Dam

2

Bibbulmun Track, North of Collie

Length: *8 km return.*
Grade: *2.*
Walk time: *3-4 hours.*

This walk takes you along a section of the newly realigned 950-kilometre-long Bibbulmun Track. You can park your car at Harris Dam picnic site, then walk to a campsite purpose-built for long-distance walkers on the Bibbulmun Track and return via the same route. The trail features views over the dam and takes you through some attractive jarrah forest.

1. Heading north-east from the car park, cross Harris River via a footbridge.
2. After the river crossing you begin to ascend through an area of water bush (*Bossiaea aquifolium*), a common member of the pea family. Its leaves have prominent spiny-toothed margins and are arranged in opposite pairs along the stem.
3. Cross an old vehicle track, then turn left via the Waugal-marked walktrail and then left again onto a vehicle track. This track takes you to the shores of Lake Ballingall, formed by the damming of the Harris River.
4. Follow the vehicle track and a 50 metre section of walktrail for a short distance around the shore of the lake.
5. Leaving the dam, near the (gravel) Norm Road, by means of the Waugal-marked walktrail, you will soon cross over a vehicle track.
6. Turn right onto an old vehicle track to reach the Harris Dam campsite, one of 46 three-sided timber sleeping shelters spaced between 10 and 20 kilometres apart, that have been erected on the new Bibbulmun Track. You may spend some time resting here, before turning back to retrace your steps.

Where is it? *About 20 km north of Collie on the Collie Tallanalla Road.*
Travelling time: *15 minutes from Collie.*
Facilities: *Barbecues, tables, boardwalk, toilets, timber shelter.*
Best season: *All year.*

Jesse Brampton and Annie Keating

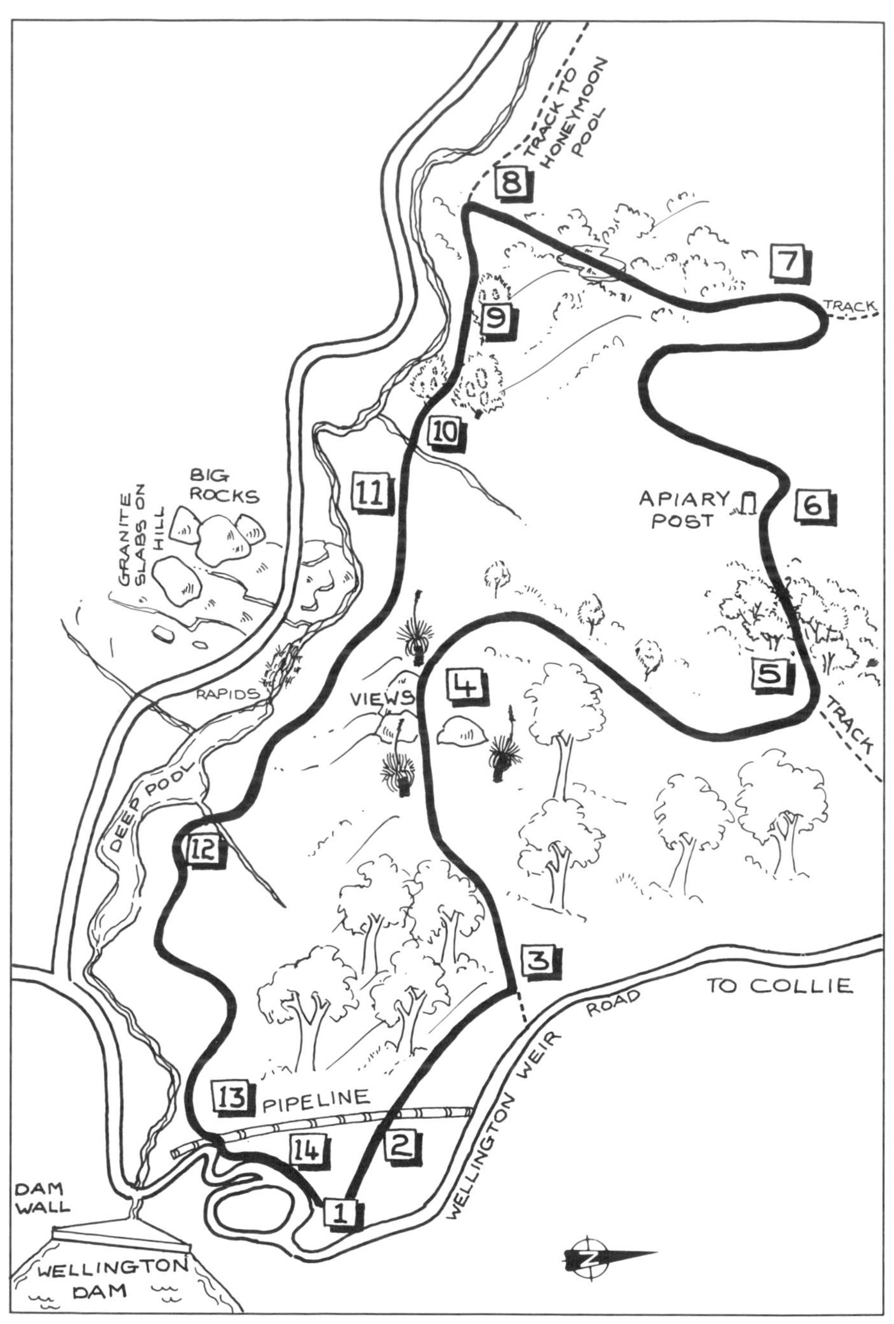
TRACK TO HONEYMOON POOL
8
7
TRACK
9
10
11
BIG ROCKS
GRANITE SLABS ON HILL
APIARY POST
6
5
TRACK
RAPIDS
VIEWS
4
DEEP POOL
12
3
TO COLLIE
ROAD
WELLINGTON WEIR
13
PIPELINE
14
2
1
DAM WALL
WELLINGTON DAM

Sika Circuit

3

Lennard Conservation Park, Collie

Length: *9.4 km.*
Grade: *4.*
Walk time: *4 hours.*

The circuit, which was once part of the Bibbulmun Track (now realigned), passes through mature jarrah and blackbutt forests and gives excellent views of the Collie River valley. The track follows the river for part of the way, passing rock outcrops, deep pools and several rapids, and is steep.

1. Begin the walk just north of the kiosk at Wellington Dam. The walk commences in a disturbed area that contains a number of weeds, including introduced wattles, then makes its way uphill.
2. You soon cross the dam pipeline. The water is now too salty for drinking, but is still used for industrial and agricultural purposes. The trail traverses open jarrah and marri woodland. Birds such as thornbills may be heard.
3. Turn left onto what is probably an old railway formation, built decades ago to facilitate logging operations. To the left, the hill slopes steeply down to the Collie River. A big winch on the carriage was typically used to haul the logs upslope.
4. You will pass an open area dotted with granite and blackboys that has sweeping views of Mount Lennard. Holly-leaved hovea (*Hovea chorizemifolia*), which has bright purple pea-shaped flowers and prickly-toothed leaves also grows here, as do a number of small snottygobble trees (*Persoonia longifolia*). Make your way around two large logs, which have fallen across the track.
5. Cross another track and traverse a dense patch of karri hazel (*Trymalium floribundum*). Termite mounds are prolific here and diggings and small oval droppings can often be seen at their base. These are the tell tale signs of one of our most intriguing and secretive mammals - the echidna.
6. A white "Apiary" post, used to denote an area used by beekeepers, can be seen along the left hand side of the track.
7. After crossing another track, which makes a sharp turn, you begin the descent down to the river. The track passes through dense glades of waterbush, traverses a small area of open granite and skirts a log that has fallen across the track.
8. After negotiating another area of thick waterbush, you will reach the old Bibbulmun Track grid point 16F, which marks the left hand turn back along the Collie River.

9. The next section of track passes through dense thickets of riverine vegetation. You will soon enjoy your first views of the river, where you should be able to discern the tall, grey-barked river banksia (*Banksia seminuda*). Introduced trout and perch now inhabit the Collie River and are sought after by anglers.
10. Cross over a stream.
11. You will soon hear the rapids and should be able to see the bare granite on the hill above them, which marks a popular recreation site known as Big Rocks. A little further on are the still waters of Deep Pool, from which you gain good views from a rocky vantage point. From here you head up, then down, a rocky track.
12. Cross another stream, then pass some small rapids, and head up over a large granite slab. You will soon glimpse the hydroelectric station, with good views to the dam wall.
13. The path heads back to the river, and some ancient jarrah trees, before leaving it for the last time. It passes over the pipeline seen at the beginning of the walk, and reaches the road, opposite the No.1 Pumping Station.
14. Turn left up the side of the narrow road to return to your car. Take great care, however, to avoid vehicles on their way down.

Where is it? *33 km from Collie.*
Travelling time: *20 minutes from Collie or 40 minutes from Bunbury.*
Facilities: *Toilets, kiosk, telephones.*
Best season: *All year during good weather.*

Carolyn Thomson and Peter Morris

THE BIBBULMUN TRACK

The Bibbulmun Track, a long distance walk track built in 1979 and realigned in 1988, was named after the Aboriginal people who inhabited an area south-west of Pemberton. They would walk long distances to attend ceremonial gatherings.

The Department of Conservation and Land Management (CALM) embarked on a massive realignment of the track in 1993, aimed at turning it into one of the world's great long distance walks. The realignment, when completed, will retain barely 10 per cent of the old route and add a significant South Coast extension, taking it some 180 kilometres further east to Albany. The majority of the new track will be in conservation estates.

The new Bibbulmun Track will stretch some 950 kilometres from Perth to Albany, traversing jarrah, marri, wandoo, karri and tingle forests, interspersed with coastal peppermint and heathlands. It will cross some of the most beautiful and wild areas of the South-West, and offer views and facilities unrivalled on any long distance trail in Australia. Campsites with shelters and other facilities are a key feature of the track, with 46 new sites being built between 10 and 20 kilometres apart. All sites are accessible only on foot.

The project's construction phase is in two parts. The northern half of the track, from Kalamunda to Nannup, was opened in August 1997. The southern half, from Nannup to Albany, will open a year later. Maps of the updated Bibbulmun Track, with extensive track notes, topographical maps, profiles and details of towns and places of interest are available from CALM, tourism outlets and good bookshops.

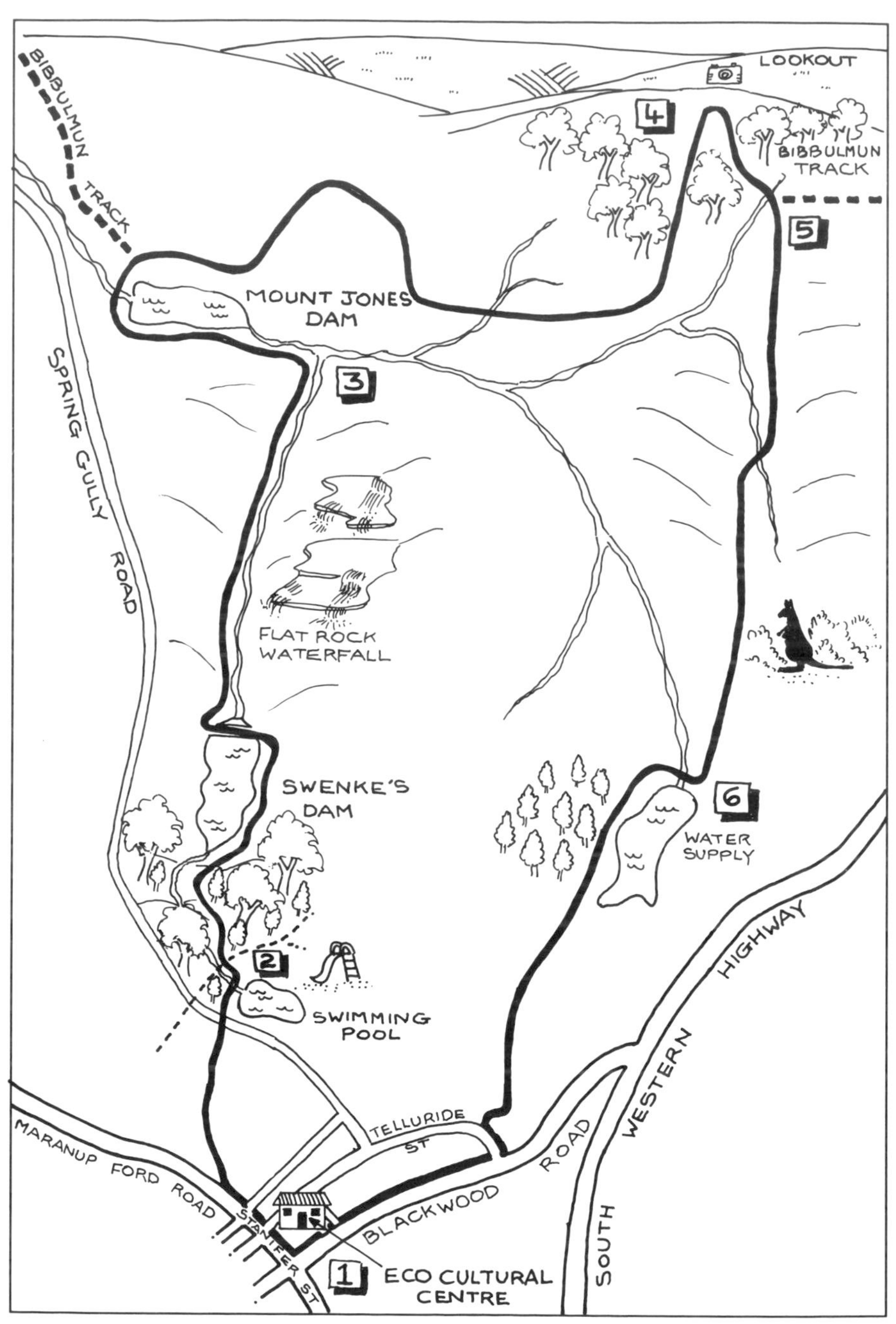

BIBBULMUN TRACK
LOOKOUT
4
BIBBULMUN TRACK
5
MOUNT JONES DAM
3
SPRING GULLY ROAD
FLAT ROCK WATERFALL
SWENKE'S DAM
6
WATER SUPPLY
2
SWIMMING POOL
SOUTH WESTERN HIGHWAY
TELLURIDE ST
MARANUP FORD ROAD
STANTFER ST
BLACKWOOD ROAD
SOUTH
1
ECO CULTURAL CENTRE

Greenbushes Loop

4

Greenbushes

Length: *15 km return.*
Grade: *3.*
Walk time: *Approximately 5 hours.*

This walk begins at the Greenbushes Eco-cultural Discovery Centre, a voluntary community organisation. It follows the Bibbulmun Track for five kilometres.

1. Follow Blackwood Road to Stanifer Street, where the trail starts. Use markers as guides to the natural swimming pool one kilometre from town.
2. Cross the road behind the toilets, climbing through young regeneration and mixed forest of jarrah and marri to Swenke's Dam, walking within sight of it, then crossing its wall to head down through Spring Gully. Note the flat granite rock areas with their special flora and little waterfalls along the way.
3. This takes you to Dumpling Gully, where you turn left, and to Mount Jones Dam. Cross the dam wall and climb some steps to join the Bibbulmun Track on its way along the dam. A climb takes you past a huge old mining ramp. The trail soon turns right and winds on, before crossing a road.
4. Eventually the track widens and leads to a lookout point over the valley. Re-enter the forest, following an old vehicle track. You will cross a creek, just before the turn to Greenbushes. Here, you leave the Bibbulmun Track, which continues straight on to Balingup.
5. Turn right to Greenbushes, then right again to cross a creek, going up the opposite side of the valley. Note the changes in vegetation which coincide with the changes of soil. There are many bird species and kangaroos are plentiful.
6. After crossing the water supply overflow, turn left, heading to the forest edge. To your right is some newly planted regeneration forest, after which a short right, then a left turn takes you to the corner of Telluride Street and Blackwood Road, and back to the Eco-Cultural Centre.

Where is it? *The turn-off to Greenbushes is about 73 km south of Bunbury on the South Western Highway.*
Travelling time: *1 hour from Bunbury.*
Facilities: *Barbecues, a playground, cold showers and toilets.*
Best season: *All year during good weather.*

Volunteers from the Greenbushes Eco-cultural Discovery Centre

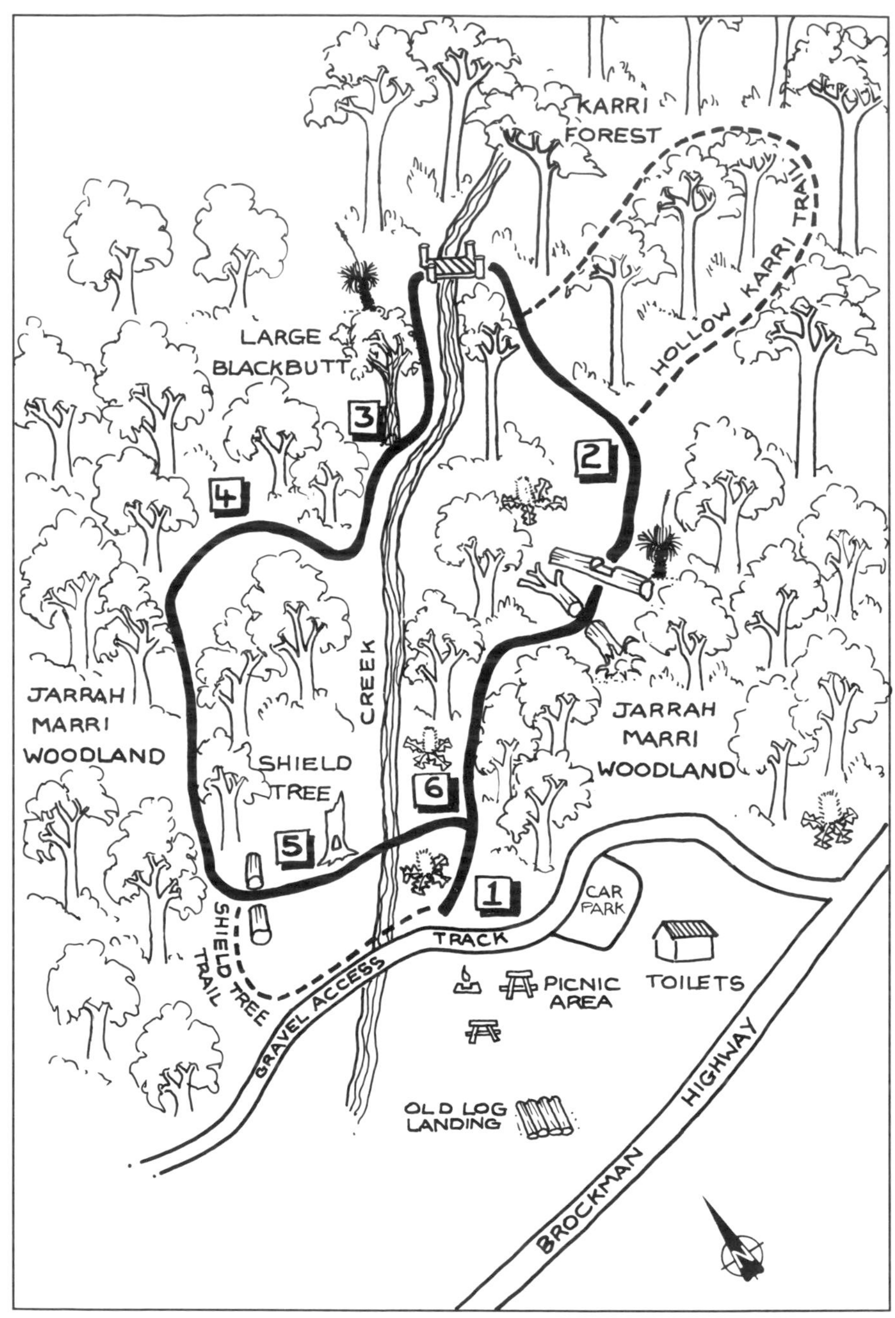
KARRI
FOREST
HOLLOW KARRI TRAIL
LARGE
BLACKBUTT
3
2
4
CREEK
JARRAH
MARRI
WOODLAND
JARRAH
MARRI
WOODLAND
SHIELD
TREE
6
5
1
CAR
PARK
SHIELD TREE TRAIL
TRACK
GRAVEL ACCESS
PICNIC
AREA
TOILETS
OLD LOG
LANDING
BROCKMAN HIGHWAY
N

Fallers Brand Trail

5

Bridgetown Jarrah Park

Length: *3.2 km.*
Grade: *2.*
Walk time: *1 hour.*

The walktrails which meander through Bridgetown Jarrah Park commemorate the early days of the South-West timber industry.

1. Make your way from the car park to the beginning of the walk. The first part of the trail is set in jarrah and marri woodland. Honeybush, yellow flags (*Patersonia*), blackboy, bull banksia (*Banksia grandis*) and snottygobble (*Persoonia longifolia*) form part of the understorey.
2. The trail moves into an area of karri (*Eucalyptus diversicolor*) and a sign indicates the turn-off to the Hollow Karri Trail. While you are still in the karri-dominated area you cross a small bridge and then have to climb under a large marri that has fallen across the trail.
3. Before long you will come to a large blackbutt (*Eucalyptus patens*) tree. Though blackbutt looks similar to jarrah it has rough grey to greyish-brown furrowed bark (the bark of jarrah is a similar colour but has vertical grooves). Blackbutt also has shorter and broader bud caps and slightly smaller fruits than jarrah. For a while the trail continues through an area of young blackbutt.
4. The trail again enters an area of jarrah/marri woodland and, before long, intersects with the Shield Tree Trail. Turn left to continue along the Fallers Brand Trail.
5. The Shield Tree is on the left side of the trail. It was part of the system of one mile grids into which the forest was divided. This system of mapping was introduced to forest management in 1924. Within each grid, "reference trees" were marked with a shield cut into the heartwood and engraved with the grid identification.
6. Turn left when the trail again branches, to return to the picnic area and car park.

Where is it? *25 km west of Bridgetown, along Brockman Highway. Bridgetown Jarrah Park is on the north side of the road, just before Sears Road.*
Travelling time: *20 minutes from Bridgetown.*
Facilities: *Picnic tables, fireplaces, information panels, toilets.*
Best season: *Spring for wildflowers.*

Carolyn Thomson and Peter Dans

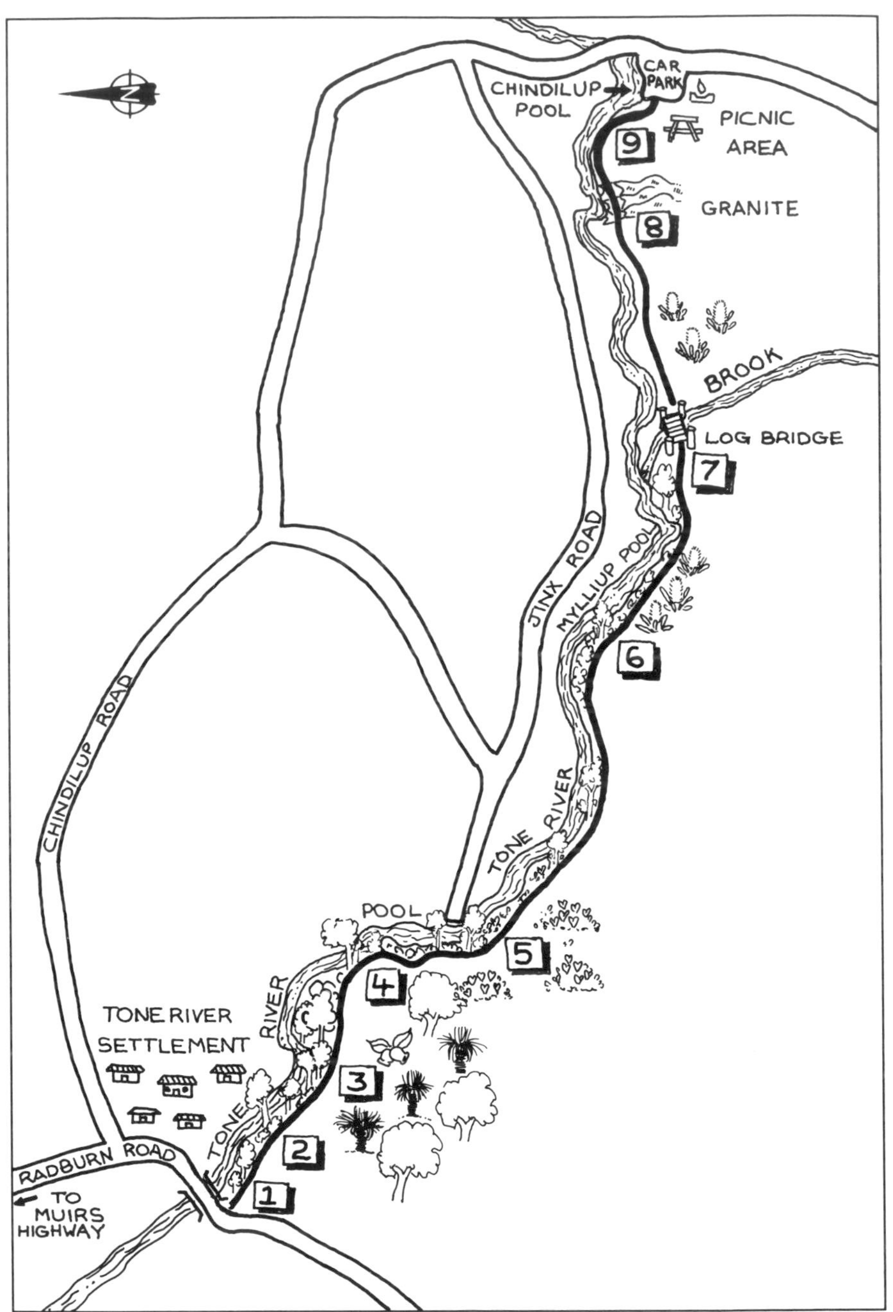
CHINDILUP POOL
CAR PARK
PICNIC AREA
9
GRANITE
8
BROOK
LOG BRIDGE
7
JINX ROAD
MYLLIUP POOL
6
CHINDILUP ROAD
TONE RIVER
POOL
5
4
TONE RIVER SETTLEMENT
RIVER
3
TONE
2
RADBURN ROAD
1
TO MUIRS HIGHWAY

Maxwell Trail

Manjimup District

Length: *14 km return (7 km one way).*
Grade: *3.*
Walk time: *5½ hours.*

This delightful walk through jarrah and flooded gum communities is adjacent to the Tone River, and lies between the Tone River Settlement and Chindilup Pool. It is recommended as a day walk. To halve the walk, you can have someone meet you at Chindilup Pool with a vehicle. Sturdy footwear is strongly suggested. During the walk, you can see many birds and animals, or signs of their presence. Startled kangaroos are often heard crashing through the understorey.

1. Just past the settlement, a bridge crosses the Tone River. The starting point is 50 metres past the bridge, on the left. Walktrail markers and yellow arrows show the way.
2. About 400 metres along the track is a gravel clearing, the site of the Radburn Mill, which operated between 1952 and 1978. Numerous debris can still be seen.
3. Pick up the track at the far end of the clearing close to the river. After a short walk, the trail diverts from the water's edge and plunges through attractive woodland dominated by jarrah (*Eucalyptus marginata*) and marri trees. Marri and other bloodwoods were once widely regarded as eucalypts, but scientists have recently placed them in a new genus, so marri is now known by the scientific name *Corymbia calophylla*. The bark of marri forms a lumpy criss-cross pattern, and often has dark red gum oozing from old wounds. Jarrah bark has a more stringy appearance and contains deep vertical grooves. Snottygobble trees (*Persoonia longifolia*), with reddish flaky bark and longish narrow leaves, are found in the understorey. There are numerous blackboys.
4. After about two kilometres, the trail takes you back to the edge of the river, and a fairly deep pool. The path skirts the dense riverine vegetation to take you to the other end of the pool.
5. The river again disappears from view as the trail weaves through areas of heartleaf poison (*Gastrolobium bilobum*). This plant has leaves, shaped like a narrow heart, clustered in whorls and yellowish-orange and red pea-shaped flowers. The plants contain fluoracetate, the same compound which is manufactured synthetically into 1080, a poison used to kill rabbits and foxes. Native animals evolved alongside the poison plants and are largely immune to the toxin.
6. About four kilometres along the track is the Mylliup Pool, with river banksia

(*Banksia seminuda*) growing near its edge. This species is one of the taller banksias and has greyish-green leaves and hard, fissured grey bark. Keep an eye and ear open for noisy birds and chirruping frogs.

7. A log bridge crosses a tributary to the river and a little further onwards is another large patch of river banksia. Birds, such as ducks and grey fantails, are occasionally seen.
8. About one kilometre from Chindilup Pool, several open areas of granite slope down to the water's edge.
9. You soon reach paperbarks fringing a rocky pool - the edge of the scenic Chindilup Pool. There are picnic tables and a trailhead sign about 50 metres west of the car park. From here you have the option of returning via Jinx Road or back along the same route.

Where is it? *Travel east along the Muir Highway for about 40 km, then turn right onto Radburn Road to reach Tone River Settlement.*
Travelling time: *40 minutes from Manjimup.*
Facilities: *Picnic tables and barbecues.*
Best season: *Spring and early summer for wildflowers.*

Carolyn Thomson and Peter Dans

The Limestone Coast Walks 7 - 18

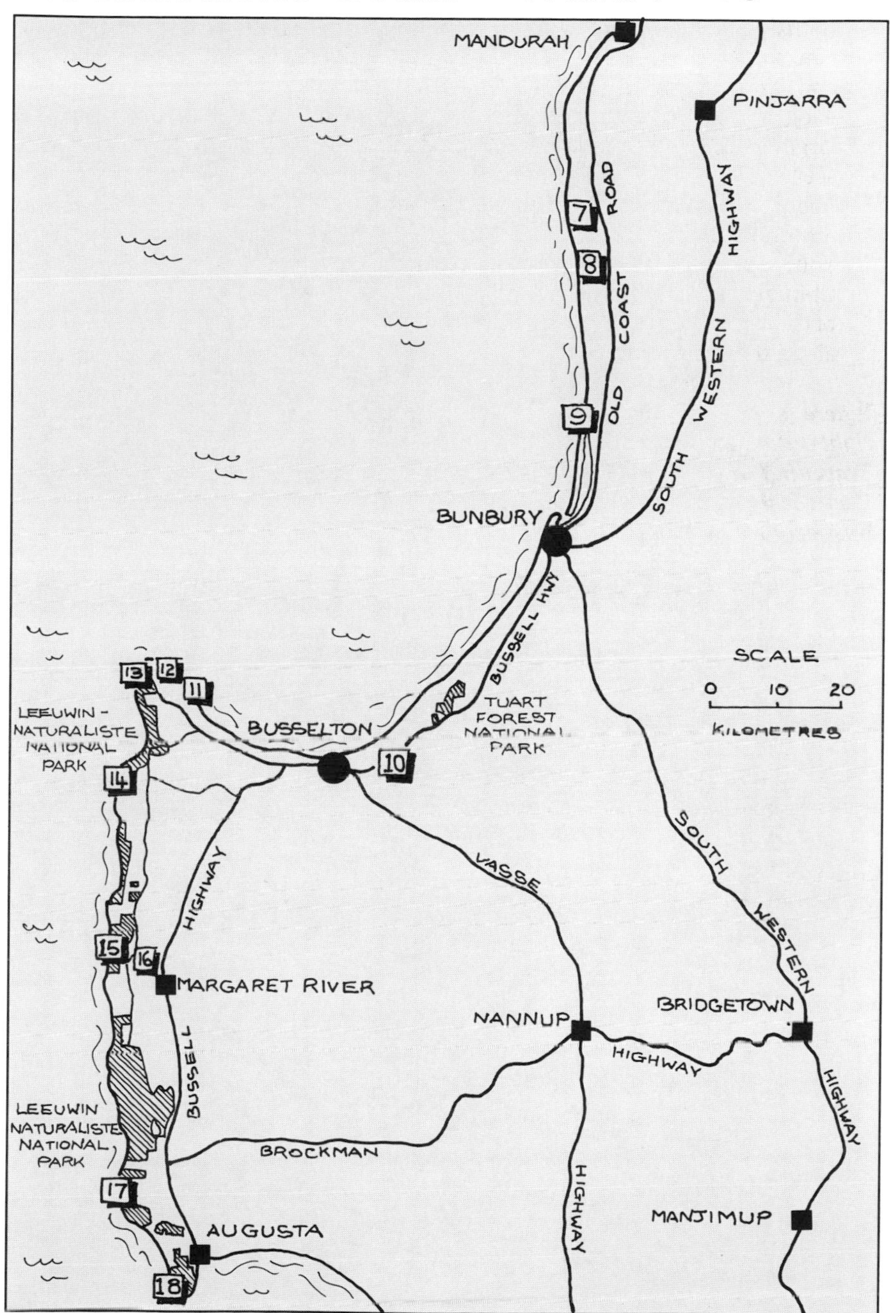

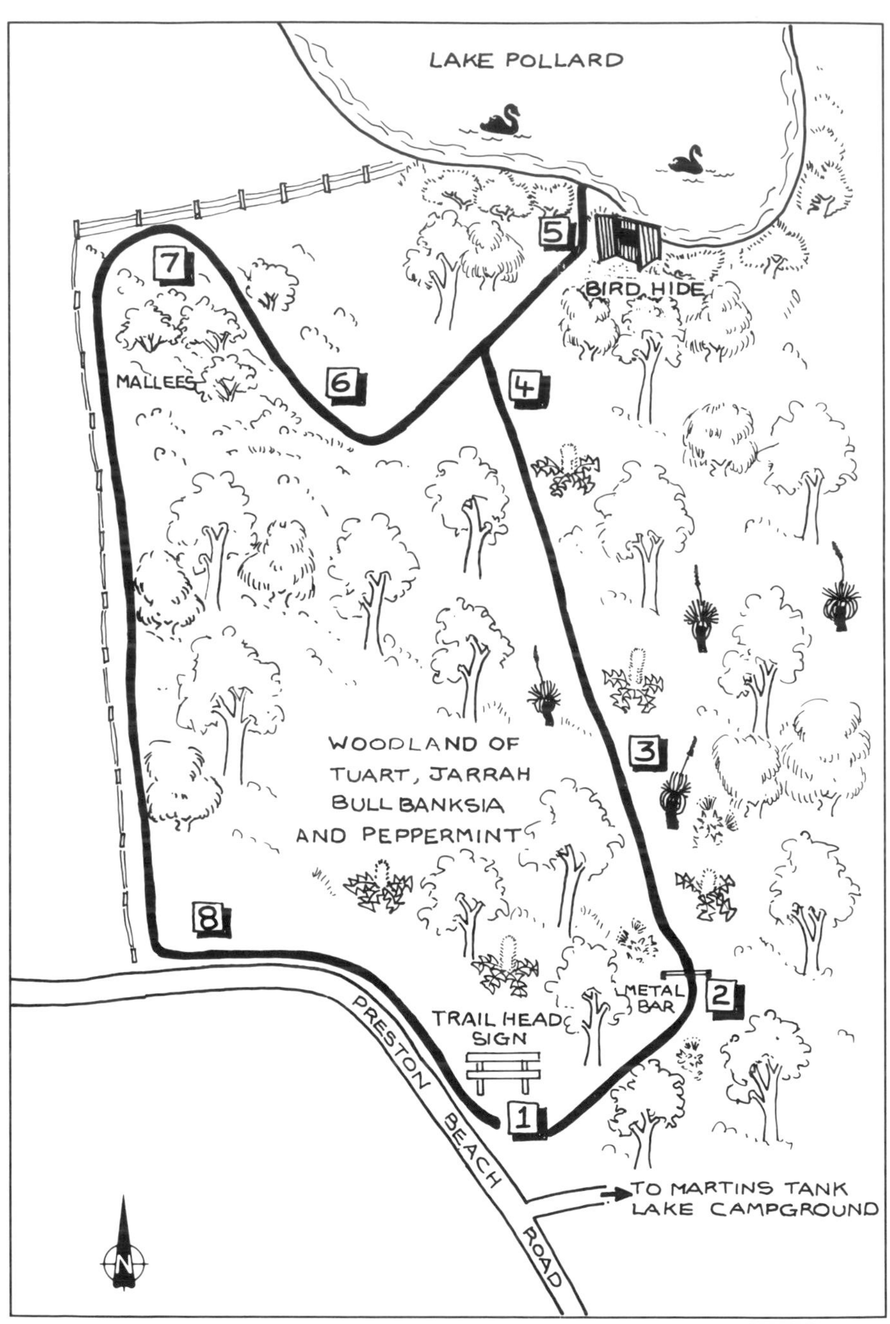
LAKE POLLARD
5
BIRD HIDE
7
MALLEES
6
4
WOODLAND OF
TUART, JARRAH
BULL BANKSIA
AND PEPPERMINT
3
8
METAL
BAR
2
TRAIL HEAD
SIGN
1
PRESTON BEACH ROAD
TO MARTINS TANK
LAKE CAMPGROUND
N

Lake Pollard Trail

7

Yalgorup National Park

Length: *6 km.*
Grade: *2.*
Walk time: *2 hours.*

Lake Pollard is renowned for its high numbers of black swans between October and March. The walk begins at the entrance to Martins Tank campground on Preston Beach Road.

1. Parrotbush (*Dryandra sessilis*), a shrub or small tree with prickly fan-shaped leaves and cream to yellow domed flower heads, grows at the start of the trail and in dense thickets across the road from the trailhead sign. However, a woodland of jarrah (*Eucalyptus marginata*), tuart (*E. gomphocephala*), peppermint (*Agonis flexuosa*) and bull banksia (*Banksia grandis*) predominates through most of the walk. Bull banksia is easily distinguished from other banksias by its larger flowers and leaves, which have deeply cut triangular lobes.
2. After about 15 minutes, turn left and step over a metal bar that prevents vehicles from entering the trail. Here, cockies tongues (*Templetonia retusa*) flower profusely from May to December. The magnificent red or pinkish-red flower of this species has a long wing petal and a distinctive long, narrow standard petal which is bent abruptly back, giving it the appearance of a cockatoo's head. If you are walking in the morning, watch for signs of animal tracks in the sandy path. You should be able to distinguish tracks of grey kangaroos or brush wallabies as well as bandicoot and possibly echidna diggings. Chuditch, brushtail possums and water rats are also known to occur in the park.
3. Other plants seen along the track include blackboys, zamia palms, prickly moses (*Acacia pulchella*) and the somewhat unkempt and usually multi-stemmed Christmas tree (*Nuytsia floribunda*), which most people rarely notice until its brilliant gold blooms appear in December.
4. On reaching a T-junction, a signpost with a yellow pointer indicates that you should turn right. The woodland is at first composed mostly of tuart and peppermint, but soon the first paperbarks indicate the close proximity of the lakes. Finally the tuarts are replaced by paperbarks, cockle shells litter the path and water can be seen between the trees.
5. Turn left when you reach a sign that advises walkers that the path does not circumnavigate the lake, and you will see the bird hide and vistas of Lake Pollard. Black swans live in high numbers here from October to March, when they graze

on extensive growths of stoneworts (musk grasses). Along the lake is a fringe of attractively gnarled and stunted, white-barked saltwater paperbarks (*Melaleuca cuticularis*).

6. Having returned to the T-junction, the adventurous will travel straight ahead (turn left and retrace your steps to return via the flatter route). Follow the trail to the right and, before long, there is a low heathland of hakea, parrotbush and cockies tongue on your left and woodland on your right.
7. When you reach the fence, turn left and climb up the steep firebreak for a magnificent vista over Lake Pollard. At the top of the hill, two rare mallees cling to the rocky hill top. The smaller rough-barked Fremantle mallee (*Eucalyptus foecunda*) has bright orange buds and white flowers, whilst the rarer limestone mallee (*E. petrensis*) has smooth, shiny bark and creamy yellow flowers. Continue to follow the fenceline back to Preston Beach Road.
8. As you walk back to the starting point along Preston Beach Road (North) look out for the kangaroo paws along the roadside.

Where is it? *50 km south of Mandurah.*
Travelling time: *About 40 minutes from Mandurah or Bunbury.*
Facilities: *There are barbecues, tables, toilets and firewood at nearby Martins Tank camping ground.*
Best season: *Black swans are a feature of the lake from October to March.*

Steve Dutton, Carolyn Thomson and Mitzi Vance

YALGORUP LAKES

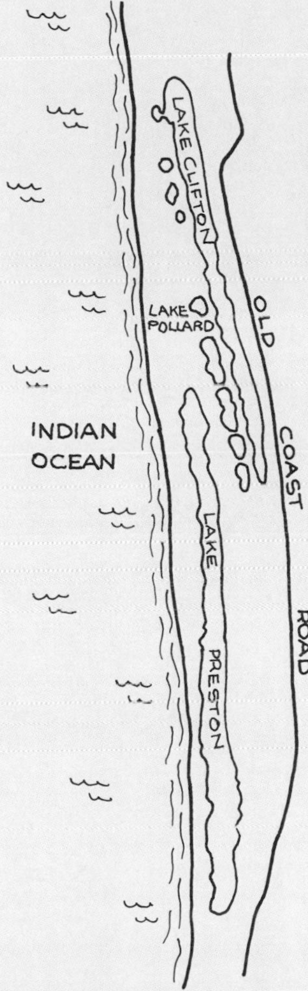

Yalgorup National Park lies on the western edge of the Swan Coastal Plain, just south of the new Dawesville Channel near Mandurah. The name is derived from two Nyoongar Aboriginal words; yalgor, meaning 'a swamp or lake', and up, a suffix meaning 'a place', an appropriate name as the park protects 10 lakes that run in a chain.

The lakes lie in the depressions between a series of coastal dunes. Reflecting this underlying structure, the ten lakes form three distinctive lines parallel to the coast. Lake Preston is extremely elongated and lies closest to the coast. The lakes behind the next ridge are far more broken, comprising (from north to south): Swan Pond, Duck Pond, Boundary Lake, Lake Pollard, Martins Tank Lake, Lake Yalgorup, Lake Hayward and Newnham Lake. Lake Clifton is the furthest from the coast and the nearest to the Old Coast Road. It too is extremely elongated.

The Yalgorup lake system is so significant for waterbirds that it is recognised under the international Ramsar Convention (named after the place where it was signed in Iran). The lakes provide important habitat for the international transequatorial waders that migrate from the northern hemisphere. These waders include the bar-tailed godwit, red-necked stint, greenshank, red knot, whimbrel and three species of sandpiper. Other waterbirds that use the lakes include the banded and black-winged stilts, red-necked avocet, hooded and red-capped plovers, Australian pelican and coot.

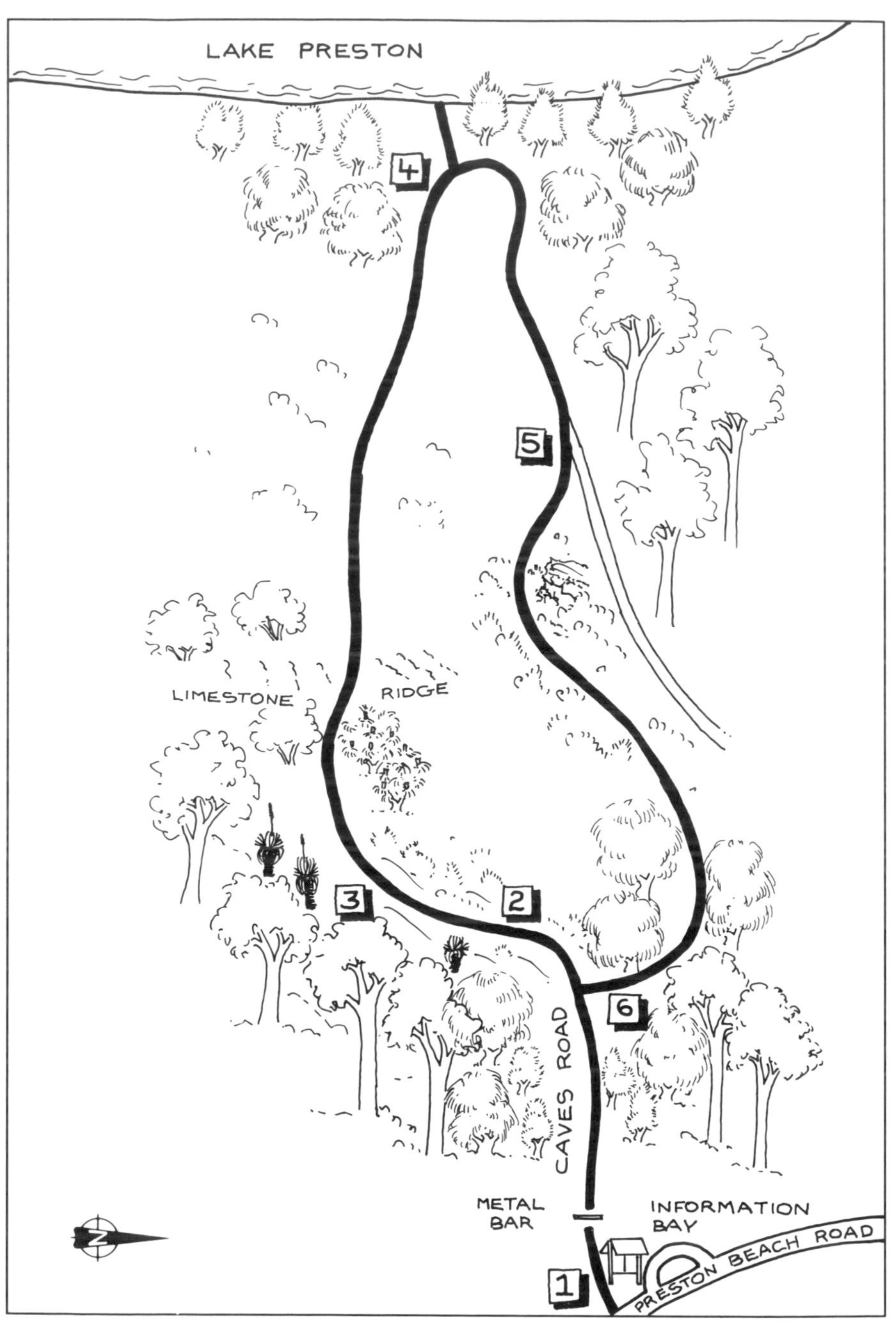

LAKE PRESTON
4
5
LIMESTONE
RIDGE
3
2
6
CAVES ROAD
METAL
BAR
INFORMATION
BAY
1
PRESTON BEACH ROAD
N

Heathlands Walk

8

Yalgorup National Park

Length: *4.5 km.*
Grade: *2*
Walk time: *1½ hours.*

This walk explores the many different vegetation types of Yalgorup National Park, from the towering tuarts to the delicate flowers of the limestone ridges.

1. Begin at the information bay on Preston Beach Road and head west along the track signposted as Caves Road. This refers to the limestone tunnels or shafts discovered here in the 1940s, which are now largely derelict.
2. As you turn left and begin to climb, the understorey of the woodland on your left thins and blackboys stand tall and proud amongst the forest. On the other side of the track, where the soils are shallower and the trees cannot grow, there is a scrubland of wattles, hakeas, grevilleas and other plants.
3. As you near the top of the rise, some swamp banksia (*Banksia littoralis*) grows in the lee of the hill. On the hill top, limestone mallees (*Eucalyptus petrensis*) and Fremantle mallees (*E. foecunda*) cling to the limestone outcrops. Enjoy the view over Lake Preston, which extends 20 kilometres south to Myalup.
4. When you reach the next marker you can take a small detour to the lake edge through the fringing thicket of swamp paperbark (*Melaleuca cuticularis*). Back at the marker, you are surrounded by thick peppermints. If you look carefully, as you continue, you may see a nest-like collection of small weaved sticks high up in the branches, called a drey. It is made by the rare western ringtail possum, which has successfully been reintroduced into this area. The track turns east and, after you leave the peppermints again, you re-enter the tuart woodland.
5. A totem indicates that the path leaves the track and winds off to the right, and you travel through thicker scrubland, around a small outcrop, then drop back into the cool peppermints once more, before rejoining the track.
6. The marker indicates to turn left onto the track, which returns to the start.

Where is it? *50 km south of Mandurah.*
Travelling time: *40 minutes from Bunbury or Mandurah.*
Facilities: *Barbecues, tables and toilets are at nearby Hayward Lake picnic site.*
Best season: *Late winter and spring for wildflowers.*

Steve Dutton

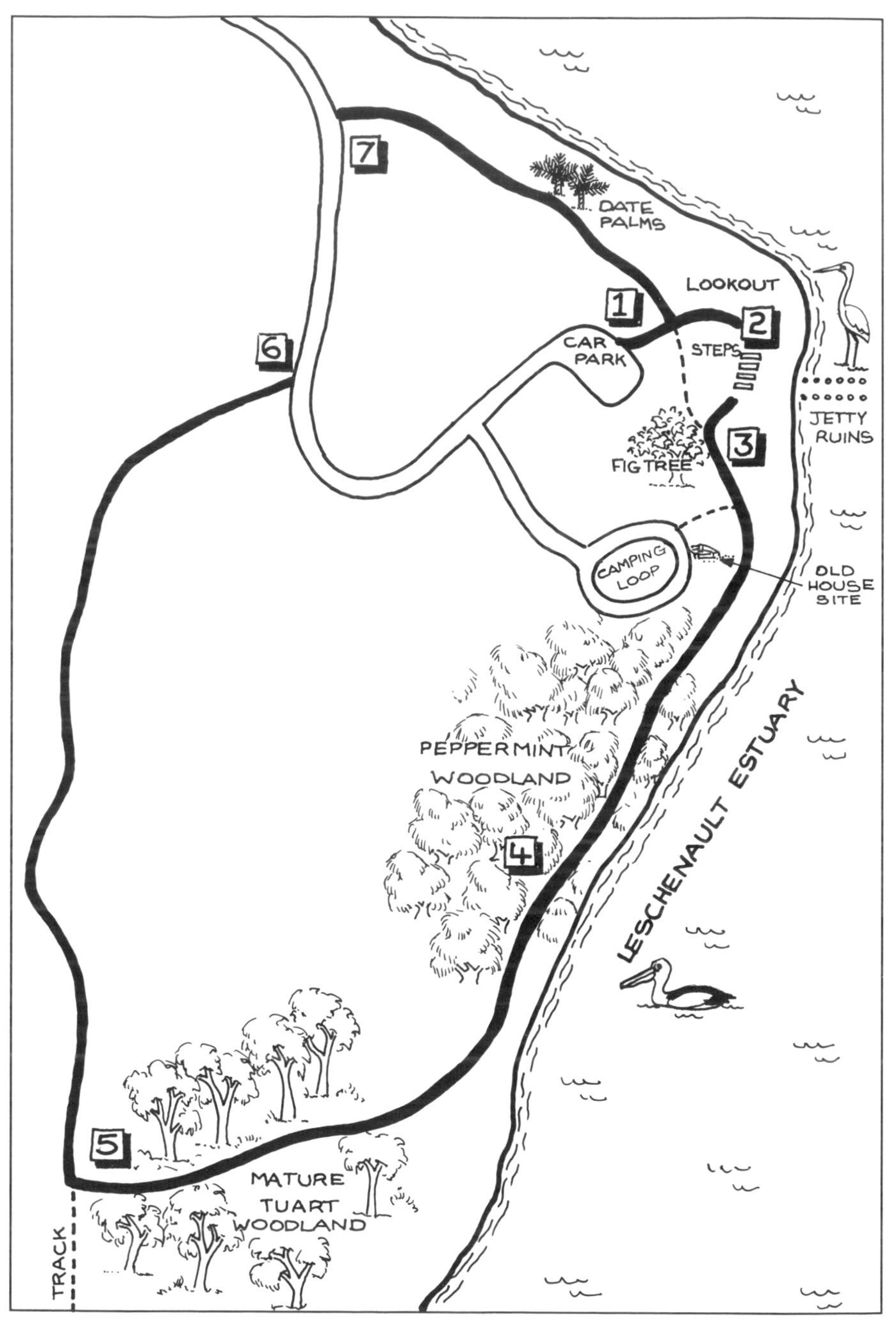
7
DATE
PALMS
LOOKOUT
1
2
6
CAR
PARK
STEPS
JETTY
RUINS
3
FIGTREE
CAMPING
LOOP
OLD
HOUSE
SITE
LESCHENAULT ESTUARY
PEPPERMINT
WOODLAND
4
5
MATURE
TUART
WOODLAND
TRACK

Belvidere Estuary Walk

9

Leschenault Peninsula Conservation Park

Length: *4 km.*
Grade: *2.*
Walk time: *$1^1/_2$ hours.*

The 11-kilometre-long Leschenault Peninsula Conservation Park is opposite Australind, lying on the other side of the estuary. Most of the park is closed to vehicular traffic, and you can only walk or cycle in to this unique coastal area.

1. Begin at the Belvidere car park and head east.
2. You soon reach a lookout over the estuary, an important area for 62 different species of waterbird. The mosquitoes which breed in the estuary are an important food source for many of these birds.
3. After negotiating the steps, turn right along the main track, a dual use path for the shared use of walkers and cyclists. It takes you along the edge of the Leschenault Estuary.
4. The path is adjacent to dense peppermint woodland. John Boyle O'Reilly was one of 62 Irish political prisoners among 279 convicts who arrived at Fremantle in 1868. He was a member of the Fenian Movement, an organisation dedicated to achieving an independent Irish Republic. While working as a member of a convict road crew near Bunbury, O'Reilly escaped and made his way to the Leschenault Peninsula. He spent several weeks sheltering in the dense peppermint woodland on the peninsula, with the assistance of a local family, and eventually made his escape by boarding the *Gazelle,* an American whaler, on March 3, 1869. O'Reilly eventually settled in Boston, where he became a well-known humanitarian, writer, poet and orator. A monument erected to O'Reilly stands at the northern entry to Leschenault Peninsula.
5. After traversing an area of mature tuart woodland, the path intersects with another track. Take the right hand turn.
6. Turn left when you reach the park access road. From 1963 to 1990, Leschenault Peninsula was used as a disposal site for acid effluent produced as waste from the production of titanium dioxide. The effluent was pumped across the estuary in a pipeline and then into a series of ponds. The former effluent disposal sites have now been rehabilitated.
7. Turn right and return to the start point, traversing an area that has been heavily disturbed by past agricultural use. Following European settlement, the Peninsula was mostly used for stock grazing. In 1838 Thomas Little purchased 741.4

hectares on Leschenault Peninsula on behalf of Charles Robert Prinsep, and named the homestead Belvidere in honour of the Prinsep mansion in Calcutta. Little managed the property to raise horses and cattle for the Indian Army. In the late 1960s and throughout the 1970s, Belvidere became a commune for alternative lifestylers, with up to 14 houses.

Where is it? *22 km north of Bunbury and 30 km south-west of Harvey, via Buffalo Road, off the Old Coast Road.*
Travelling time: *30 minutes from Bunbury.*
Facilities: *Barbecues, tables, toilets.*
Best season: *All year.*

Peter Morris

GREAT EGRET

Great egrets (*Ardea alba*), with their long necks and somewhat lethal, pointed beaks, are one of the most elegant birds found in the South-West. They are the largest of the white herons. These long-legged waterbirds often wade around the shallow waters of Australind's Leschenault Inlet, searching for food in the mud. They may stand still for long periods watching for a likely meal, then slowly stalk their prey until the opportunity arises to snatch it. Their main food is fish but they also snack on insects, frogs and crustaceans.

The birds nest in a platform of sticks. This is placed in a tree, up to 15 metres above the ground, or in a bed of reeds. The birds are found through most of Australia, apart from arid areas in the inland. Australind, with a large and productive food source nearby, has the largest breeding colony of great egrets in the South-West. Both parents incubate between three and six eggs, and two young usually survive to fledging, which takes about six weeks.

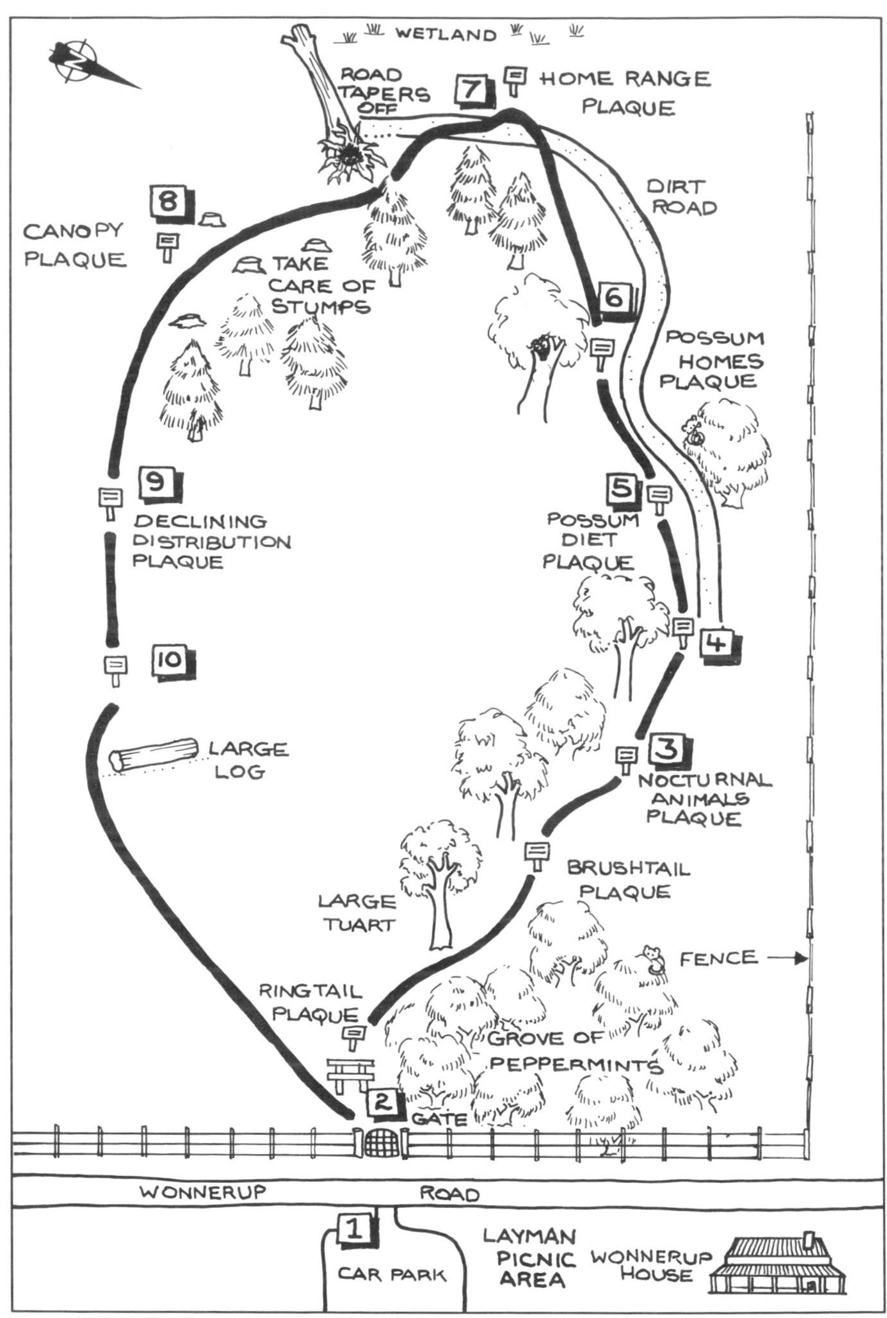
WETLAND
ROAD TAPERS OFF
7
HOME RANGE PLAQUE
8
CANOPY PLAQUE
TAKE CARE OF STUMPS
DIRT ROAD
6
POSSUM HOMES PLAQUE
9
DECLINING DISTRIBUTION PLAQUE
5
POSSUM DIET PLAQUE
4
10
LARGE LOG
3
NOCTURNAL ANIMALS PLAQUE
BRUSHTAIL PLAQUE
LARGE TUART
FENCE
RINGTAIL PLAQUE
GROVE OF PEPPERMINTS
2
GATE
WONNERUP ROAD
1
CAR PARK
LAYMAN PICNIC AREA
WONNERUP HOUSE

Possum Night Spotlighting Trail

10

Tuart Forest National Park

***Length:** 1.5 km loop.*
***Grade:** 1.*
***Walk time:** 1 hour.*

This walk is a self-guided trail designed to be completed at night with a spotlight or large torch, so as to come face-to-face with the nocturnal inhabitants of the tuart forest. This area has one of the largest populations of the rare western ringtail possum and the densest populations of brushtails ever recorded in Western Australia, and you are highly likely to see these creatures. Red reflectors on the trail markers and information plaques guide the way. Spotting the animals is up to you.

1. Begin at the Layman picnic area, on the eastern side of Wonnerup Road, just south of historic Wonnerup House. Cross to the other side of the road, taking care to avoid vehicles, and go through the gate.
2. Immediately in front of you is the trailhead sign in a grove of peppermint trees (*Agonis flexuosa*), with their weeping foliage and aromatic leaves. Nearby is the first plaque, which is about ringtail possums. See if you can spot any nearby. Following the red reflectors, make your way through peppermint and tuart (*Eucalyptus gomphocephala*) trees until you locate the plaque about brushtail possums.
3. The next plaque describes other nocturnal animals you may encounter - the wambenger (also known as the brush-tailed phascogale), tawny frogmouth and boobook owl.
4. A further plaque gives information about the breeding biology of possums.
5. Locate a fifth plaque about possum diet.
6. The next piece of information provided is about the homes built by possums. These may be placed in the hollows of trees or the animals may pile sticks to make a platform nest called a drey.
7. The trail now passes through large pine trees planted by foresters. A plaque, adjacent to a wetland, describes the typical home ranges of the ringtail and brushtail possums.
8. Negotiate your way around a fallen tree and through an area of pines that has been partially harvested. Take care to avoid remaining pine stumps. Here, locate a plaque about the use made by possums of the interlocking canopy.
9. Pass through more pines and back into peppermint trees to discover the reasons for the declining distribution of these fascinating mammals.

10. There is now only one more plaque to locate before you pass to the right of a large log to return to the trailhead and back through the gate to the car park.

Where is it? *16 km from Busselton.*
Travelling time: *10-15 minutes from Busselton.*
Facilities: *Picnic tables, barbecues, toilets and information.*
Best season: *All year during fine weather.*

Kim Williams

WESTERN RINGTAIL POSSUM

Once considered to be a subspecies of the common ringtail possum found in eastern Australia, the western ringtail possum is now regarded as a separate species. It has suffered a severe decline in recent decades but survives in reasonable numbers in a few coastal areas of peppermint woodland, particularly in the areas around Busselton and Albany. It also lives in isolated pockets of jarrah forest near Manjimup.

Western ringtail possums (*Pseudocheirus occidentalis*) have smaller rounded ears and tails with shorter fur than larger brushtail possums. Their fur is usually very dark brown, with a lighter belly. The tail, which is curled around branches as an aid in climbing, ends in a white tip. Adults weigh around one kilogram.

Ringtail possums are nocturnal and spend most of their time in the canopy, moving from one tree to another where the branches overlap. There are few hollows in peppermint trees, so here ringtails build platforms or nests, known as dreys. They are sociable and several individuals may live close together. Around Busselton, look for their dreys in the peppermints. In periods of hot weather you can occasionally see distressed individuals seeking a cooler resting spot.

Leaves, fruit and flowers form the staple diet of this animal. It appears that some ringtail possums can breed all year round and raise more than one litter in that time. Twins are not uncommon. Young stay on their pouch for several weeks and then travel on their mother's back for several more.

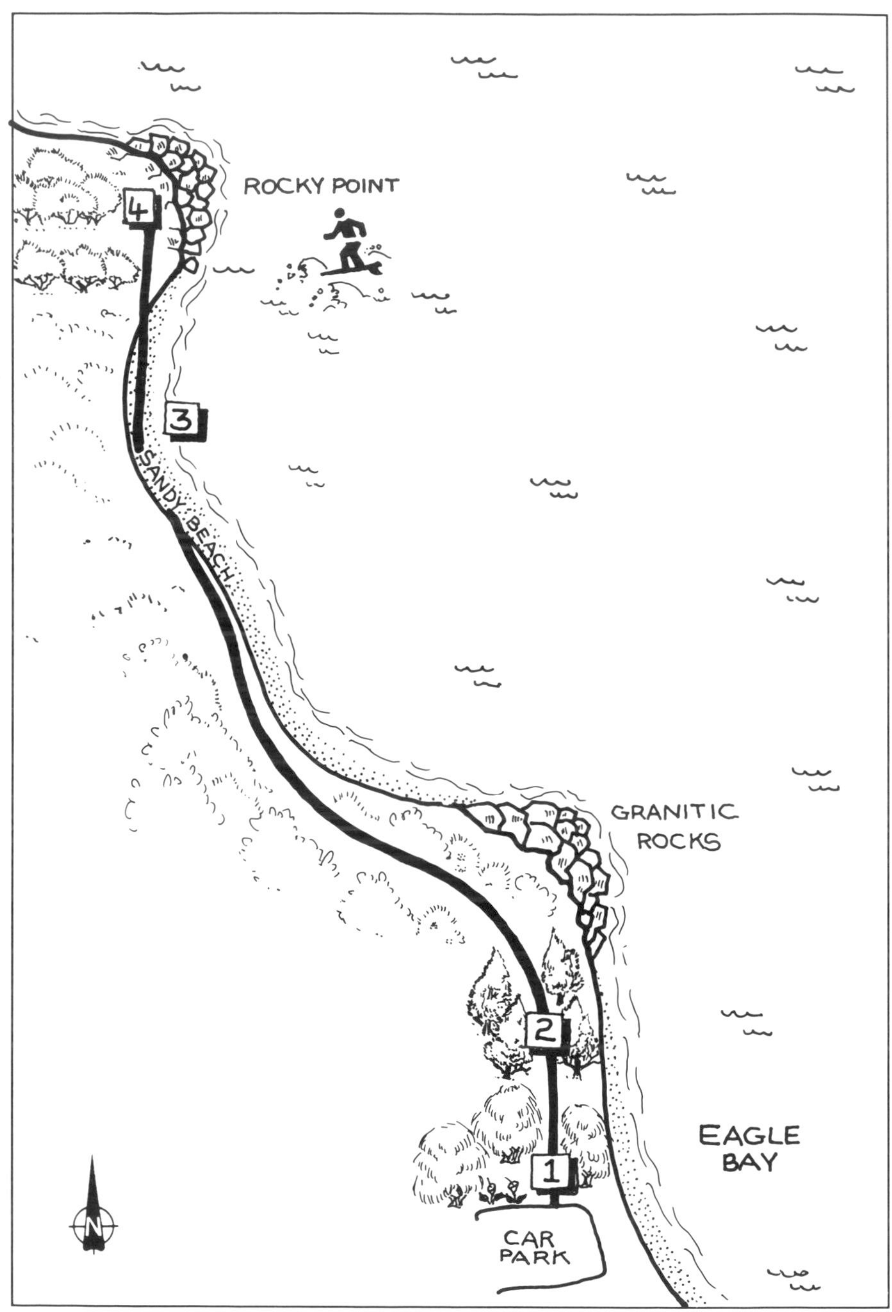
ROCKY POINT
4
3
SANDY BEACH
GRANITIC ROCKS
2
1
EAGLE BAY
CAR PARK
N

Eagle Bay to Rocky Point 11

Length: *Approximately 2 km return.*
Grade: *1.*
Walk time: *40 minutes.*

This excellent family walk begins at the most northern car park at Eagle Bay (the turn-off to the car park is near the volunteer fire brigade building on Fern Road). In summer you can enjoy blue skies and a swim, in spring there are delightful wildflowers, while in winter beachcombing is especially rewarding.

1. As you leave the car park in winter or spring, you will notice a proliferation of arum lilies, which have colonised winter wet areas throughout the Leeuwin-Naturaliste ridge. The species was introduced by early settlers as a garden plant and its seeds float down the creeks and rivers, as well as being spread by birds.
2. A number of Rottnest Island tea-trees (*Melaleuca lanceolata*) grow close to the coast. The large spreading branches of this tree have been sculpted by the salt-laden winds. Red-eyed wattle (*Acacia cyclops*) grows along the path. In late spring to early summer, when the seed pods first open, the shiny black seeds, encircled by thick orange-red stalks, resemble bloodshot eyes. Granite clawflower (*Calothamnus graniticus*) can be recognised by its red, feathery, claw-like flowers. This rare species grows only on Cape Naturaliste.
3. The final stage of the walk to Rocky Point takes you along the beach. In winter, searches should be able to turn up numerous urchins, shells and other interesting finds. Cuttlebones, which are the skeletons of cuttlefish, are numerous. See if you can find cuttlebones with teeth punctures in regular rows. These are made by dolphins, one of the main predators of cuttlefish.
4. As well as being a well-known surfing spot, Rocky Point is quite scenic, with its groves of Rottnest tea-trees and granitic rocks jutting into the ocean.

Where is it? *10 km from Dunsborough via the Cape Naturaliste Road, Eagle Bay Road and Fern Road.*
Travelling time: *5-10 minutes from Dunsborough.*
Facilities: *Single portable chemical toilet. Full toilet conveniences are located at the corner of Eagle Bay-Meelup Road and Gypsy Street, near the Eagle Bay shop. No drinking water.*

Carolyn Thomson and Peter Dans

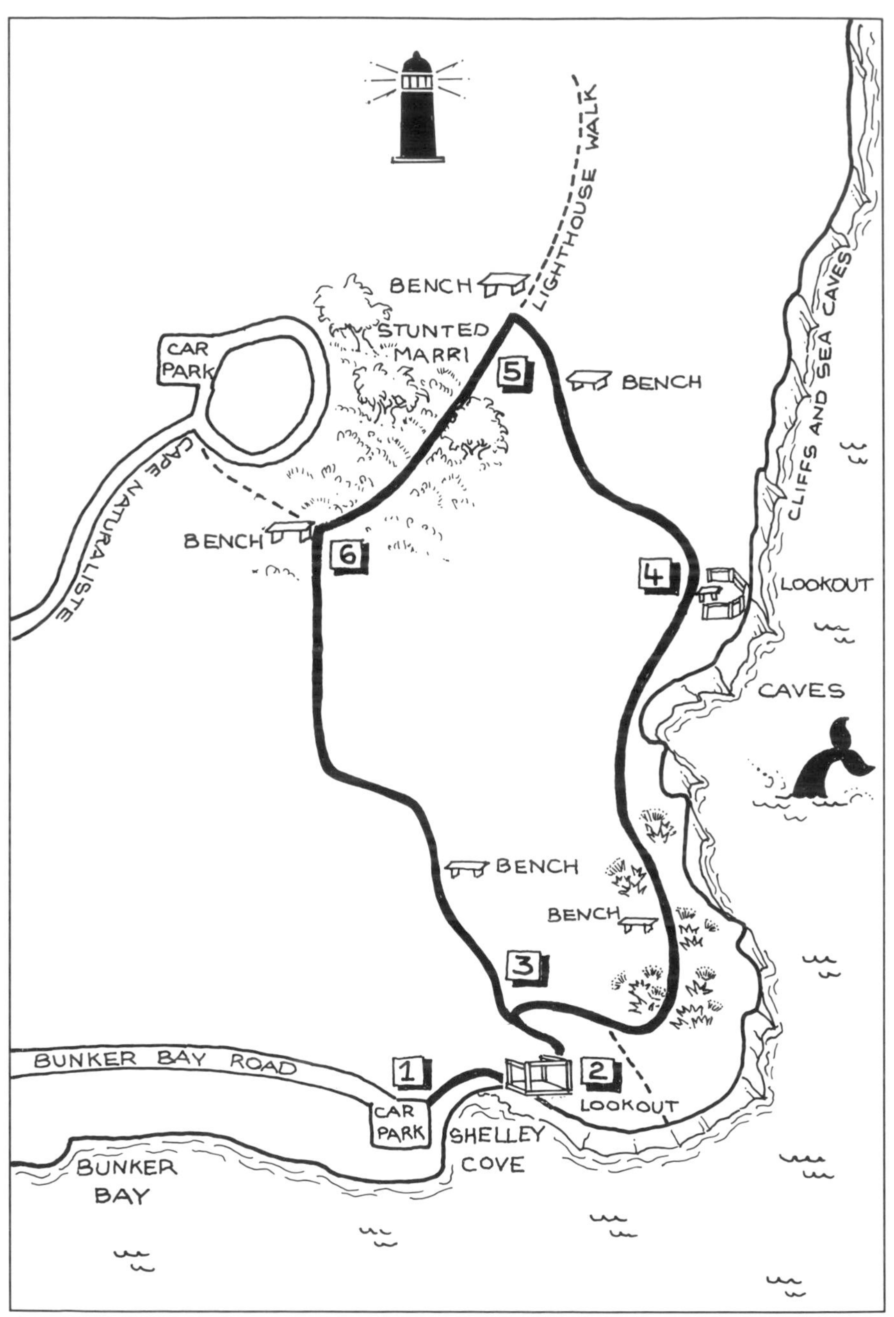
LIGHTHOUSE WALK
BENCH
STUNTED MARRI
CAR PARK
5
BENCH
CLIFFS AND SEA CAVES
CAPE NATURALISTE
BENCH
6
4
LOOKOUT
CAVES
BENCH
BENCH
3
BUNKER BAY ROAD
1
2
CAR PARK
LOOKOUT
SHELLEY COVE
BUNKER BAY

Bunker Bay

12

Leeuwin-Naturaliste National Park

Length: *2.5 km.*
Grade: *3.*
Walk time: *1 to 1½ hours.*

This track leads to the cliff edge, revealing breathtaking views of the coast.

1. Begin at the Bunker Bay car park and head north around Shelly Cove through a woodland of melaleucas.
2. The viewing platform overlooking Shelly Cove provides distant views of Geographe Bay, near Busselton. French explorer Nicolas Baudin landed in Geographe Bay in 1802, naming the bay and Cape Naturaliste after two of his ships. Sealers and whalers, mostly American, French and British, visited Australian shores in the early 1800s, but did not set up permanent settlements in WA.
3. About 100 metres up from the lookout, the track branches into two. Take the track to your right, which leads north and then east along the cliffs. The path is quite rocky, so take care. Stands of parrotbush (*Dryandra sessilis*), which has prickly fan-shaped leaves and cream or yellow flowers, grow along the path.
4. About 550 metres from where you turned off, a spur path leads to another lookout. It is a good place to see southern right whales, during winter and spring, and humpback whales, making their way south to Antarctic waters, from September to November. Both species were once hunted almost to extinction.
5. Head inland through coastal heath. In spring time colourful wildflowers abound. Turn left when you meet up with the lighthouse walk. (If you wish, turn right to loop around to the lighthouse and back to rejoin the Bunker Bay walk, adding a further 1.2 kilometres to the walk). The 20 metre high limestone lighthouse was built in 1903. Its powerful light can beam 48 kilometres out to sea on a clear night.
6. About 330 metres after joining the lighthouse walk, turn left (where the track again branches) to return to Shelly Cove and then the car park.

Where is it? *36 km from Busselton and 261 km from Perth.*
Travelling time: *25 minutes from Busselton.*
Facilities: *Tables, toilets, information.*
Best season: *All year round, but spring is best for wildflowers and whales.*

Neil Taylor

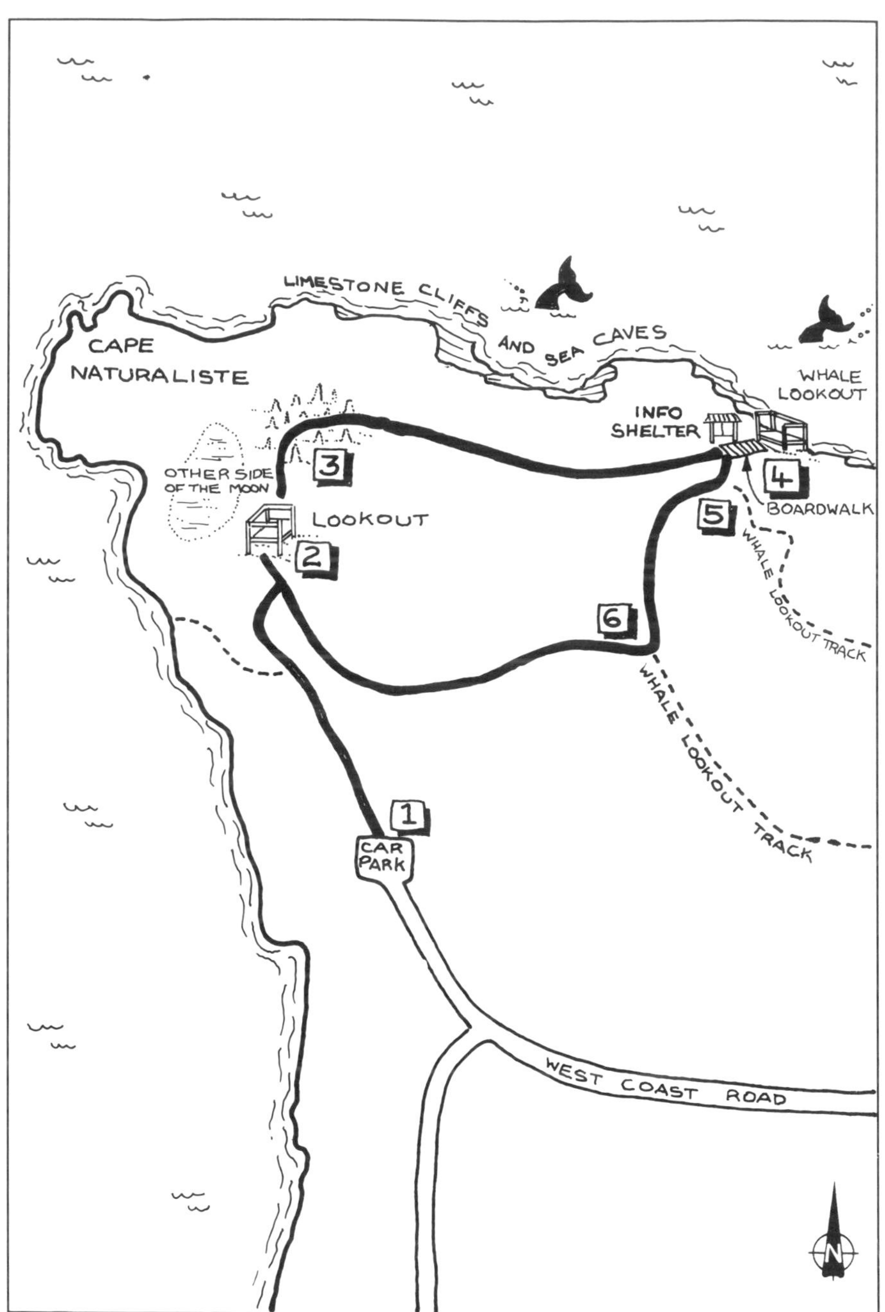
LIMESTONE CLIFFS AND SEA CAVES
CAPE NATURALISTE
WHALE LOOKOUT
INFO SHELTER
OTHER SIDE OF THE MOON
3
4
BOARDWALK
5
LOOKOUT
2
WHALE LOOKOUT TRACK
6
WHALE LOOKOUT TRACK
1
CAR PARK
WEST COAST ROAD
N

Cape Naturaliste Track

13

Leeuwin-Naturaliste National Park

Length: *3.2 km.*
Grade: *3*
Walk time: *1 to 1½ hours.*

The Cape Naturaliste Track has breathtaking coastal views and travels through small limestone 'pinnacles' en route to a stunning whale lookout. Turn off Naturaliste Terrace Road onto West Coast Road, 500 metres before the Lighthouse car park. Remain on the West Coast Road until you reach the northerly car park.

1. From the car park, walk north along a dirt track.
2. Passing a small track that leads to the coast, head to the Naturaliste Lookout. Immediately in front of you is a barren landscape known as 'The Other Side of the Moon'. Beyond it is Cape Naturaliste, named after the French ship that sailed up the WA coast in 1801. The Cape is the northernmost point of the park. To the south you can see Gull Rock and Sugarloaf Rock. On a windy day, the power of the Southern Ocean can be astounding.
3. The track continues through an area known as 'The Pinnacles', limestone projections in an area largely devoid of vegetation. Because of the rocky terrain the track is not well defined, so look carefully for markers to show the way.
4. Continue to the whale lookout over the high limestone cliffs. It is at the end of a long boardwalk. You may see southern right whales, during winter and spring, and humpback whales from September to November. Out of whale watching season, it provides panoramic coastal views and the chance to spot birds living in the area.
5. Head inland, passing through diverse coastal heath.
6. When the track branches, take the route to the right. Another turn, just before you reach the lookout at point 2, returns to the car park.

Where is it? *36 km from Busselton and 261 km from Perth.*
Travelling time: *25 minutes from Busselton.*
Facilities: *Tables, toilets, information.*
Best season: *All year round, but spring is best for wildflowers and whales.*

Neil Taylor

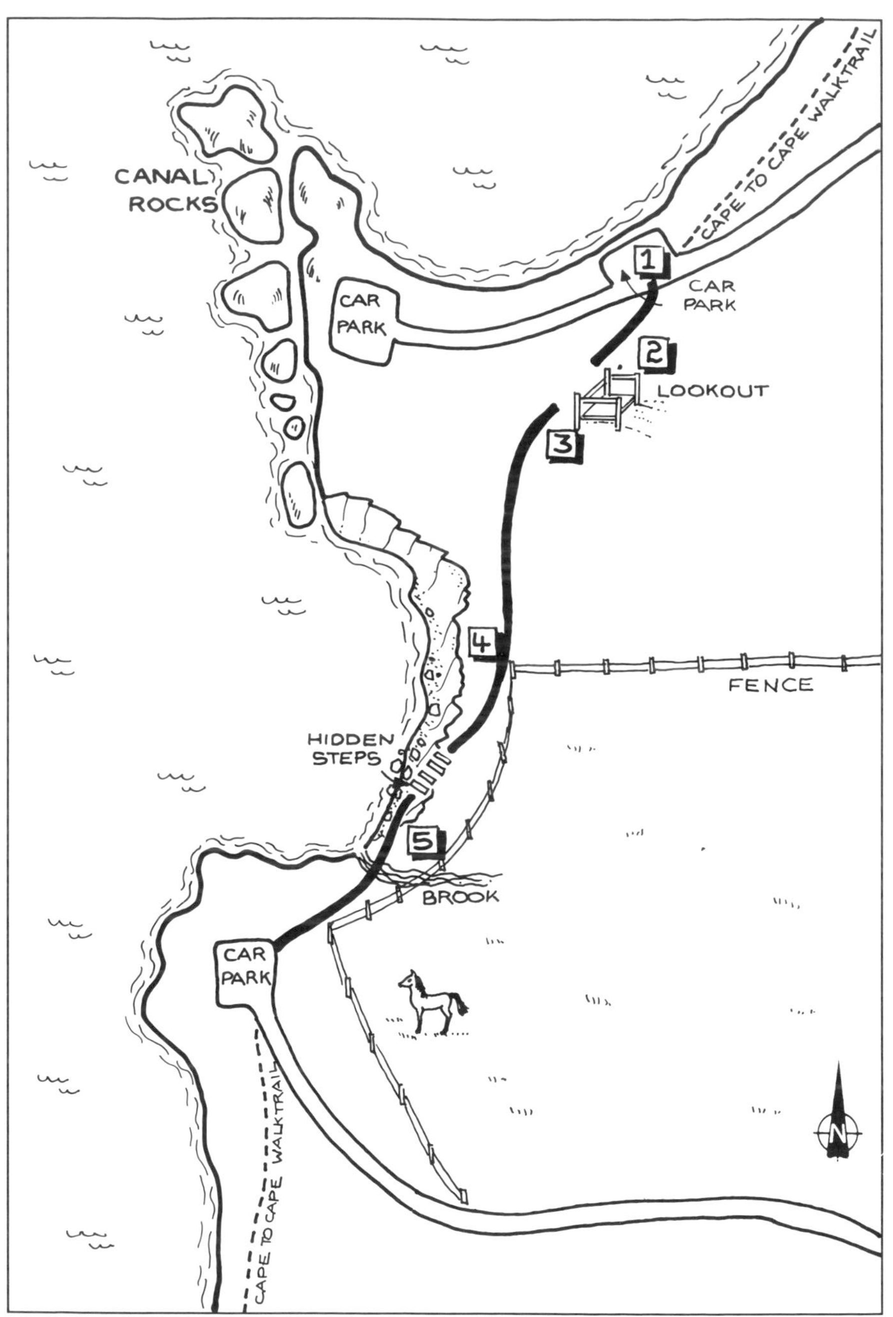

CANAL
ROCKS
CAR
PARK
CAPE TO CAPE WALKTRAIL
1
CAR
PARK
2
LOOKOUT
3
4
FENCE
HIDDEN
STEPS
5
BROOK
CAR
PARK
CAPE TO CAPE WALKTRAIL
N

Canal Rocks to Wyadup

14

Leeuwin-Naturaliste National Park

Length: *2 km one way, or 4 km return.*
Grade: *3.*
Walk time: *2 hours return.*

This walk is part of the 140-kilometre Cape to Cape Walk Track, from Cape Naturaliste to Cape Leeuwin. A brochure for Section 1 (with a total length of 18 kilometres) is available from local CALM offices and tourist outlets for a nominal fee.

1. Begin at the car park on Canal Rocks Road. Leeuwin-Naturaliste National Park had its beginnings in the 1930s. More land was gradually added to it over time and today it is nearly 16 000 hectares and the State's most visited national park.
2. Walk 200 metres to the Rotary Lookout, which has stunning views over Canal Rocks. It is thought that about 600 million years ago, the original granite rocks were subjected to a period of intense heat and pressure, causing changes in their structure and mineral composition, to form the metamorphic rock, granitic gneiss. The rocks became layered and folded, forming bands of varying hardness which tend to lie parallel to the present coastline. Bands of weaker rock have been eroded more easily by the sea, creating the spectacular canal formation. The Aboriginal name for the rocks is Winjee Sam.
3. From the lookout, a narrow rock-strewn path continues upwards over the Leeuwin-Naturaliste ridge, a geological formation of ancient granite, capped by limestone and sand dunes, which runs for the length of the park.
4. The path levels out, then descends, passing a fence. Very steep, well-hidden steps wind down to a boulder strewn beach. To the north, there are sensational views of a cliff face, where erosion is eating into the ridge.
5. The path lies just above the edge of the beach. You soon cross a brook, then follow a paddock fence back to the Wyadup car park. On reaching Wyadup, you can either retrace your steps or have someone meet you with a car.

Where is it? *8 km from Yallingup or 14 km from Dunsborough.*
Travelling time: *10 minutes from Yallingup.*
Facilities: *Toilets at nearby Canal Rocks.*
Best season: *All year during fine weather.*

Neil Taylor

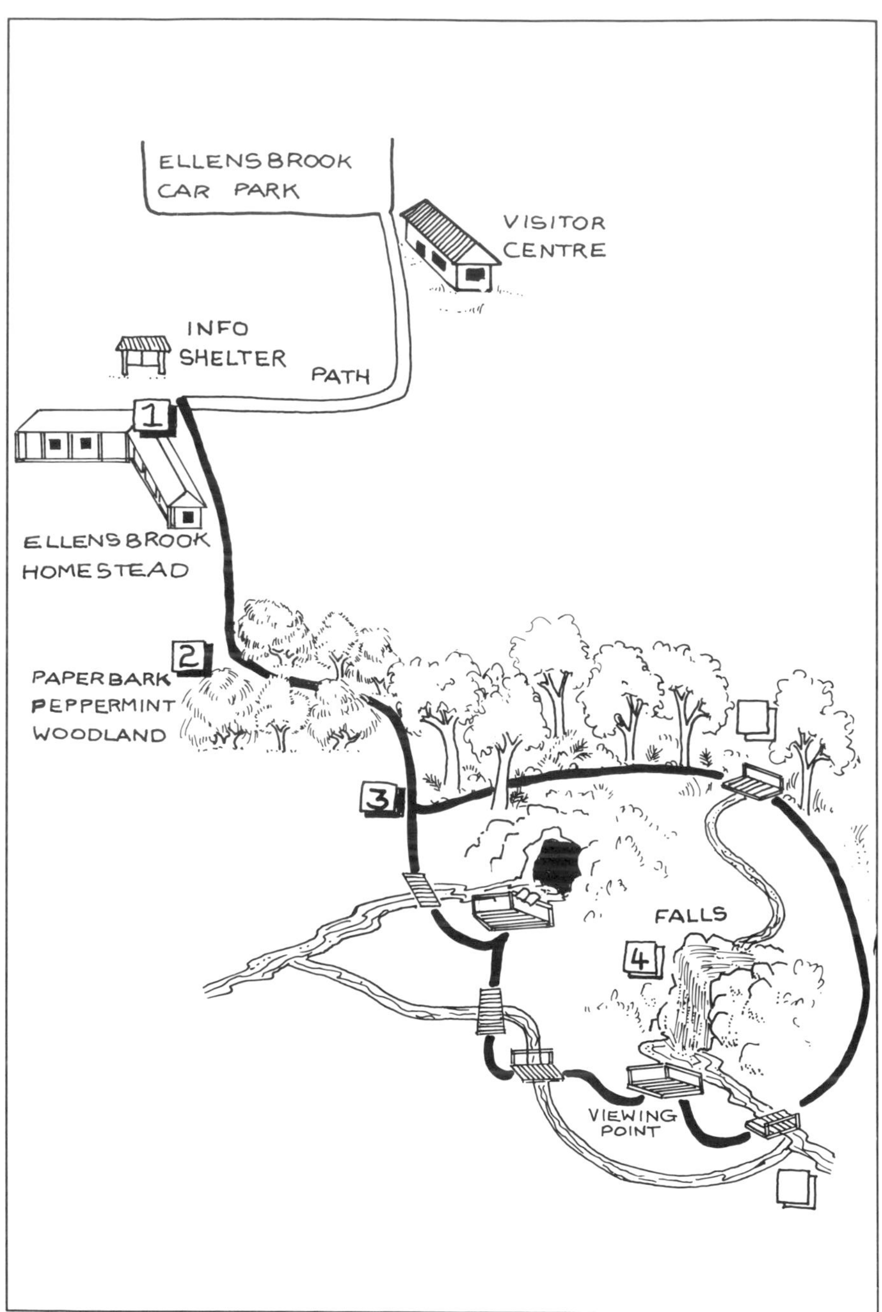
ELLENSBROOK
CAR PARK
VISITOR
CENTRE
INFO
SHELTER
PATH
1
ELLENSBROOK
HOMESTEAD
2
PAPERBARK
PEPPERMINT
WOODLAND
3
FALLS
4
VIEWING
POINT

Meekadarabee Falls

15

Leeuwin-Naturaliste National Park

Length: *2 km.*
Grade: *1.*
Walk time: *40 minutes.*

This easy walk takes visitors to Meekadarabee Falls, one of the lesser known, but surprisingly beautiful, attractions of the South-West. The trail and all facilities are accessible to the disabled.

1. The walktrail begins at Ellensbrook Homestead. Alfred Bussell arrived in Western Australia in 1830, and later pioneered the Margaret River area. In 1857 he built Ellensbrook as a home for his new bride, Ellen, out of crushed shell and limestone. He and Ellen, who was just 16, set off from Busselton on their honeymoon through the then trackless scrub of the Leeuwin-Naturaliste Peninsula. Alfred led her to the site he had chosen for their homestead, at the mouth of a small stream about 25 kilometres south of Cape Naturaliste. They lived here until 1865, when they moved to Wallcliffe House at the mouth of the Margaret River. The family lived a meagre existence, which gradually improved as they managed to sell some of their produce and build onto their one-room hut. A kitchen was added so Ellen no longer had to cook outdoors. Two of the couple's children died as infants and were buried near Ellensbrook, along with a convict helper and Alfred's brother, Charles Bussell.
2. Paperbark and peppermint trees fringe the path en route to the cave. Between July and November you may be able to see the small pink flowers of winged boronia (*Boronia alata*) growing near the path's edge. It can be recognised by its four pointed petals and glossy green leaves.
3. As you approach the waterfall, the vegetation changes abruptly to taller jarrah trees with a cool, moist understorey of ferns and other water-loving plants. A boardwalk has been built to protect the site.
4. Information panels at the small waterfall tell the story of Meekadarrabee. According to local Aboriginal people, a girl called Mitanne would spend her time exploring caves and strange places. Sometimes a boy called Nobel would accompany her. One evening Mitanne hurried back to camp and told her mother she had found Meekadarabee, the Moon's bathing place. Her grandmother was angry, as to gaze upon Meeka in the water brings death and sorrow. Mitanne had been promised to a tribal elder, but eloped with Nobel. They lived happily at Meekadarrabee, hunting at night to avoid being found. The elder sent warriors

to find Nobel and kill him. One night he stayed out hunting much longer than usual and Mitanne found him speared through the body. He died in her arms. She was taken back to the elder and forced to do all the hard work around camp until she collapsed and died.

5. The offshoot path just before the waterfall takes you to the spring behind it. After Mitanne died, the spirit of Nobel was waiting for her in the peppermint trees. They made their way to this cave and it is said that their spirit still resides here. You can see where the stream disappears into the limestone rock, which it filters through to create the waterfall on the other side.
6. A small wooden bridge takes you back over the stream to loop back to the original path. Retrace your steps to return to the homestead.

Where is it? *The turn-off to Ellensbrook Homestead, off Caves Road, is 30 km from Yallingup or 9 km from Margaret River. It lies a further 4 km along Ellensbrook Road.*
Travelling time: *20 minutes from Yallingup or 10 minutes from Margaret River.*
Facilities: *Toilets, information, historic homestead managed by the National Trust.*
Best season: *Winter and spring, when the falls are in full flow.*

Kim Williams and Carolyn Thomson

HONEY POSSUM

This tiny marsupial is highly specialised for feeding on nectar and pollen. Its long snout and brush-tipped tongue are perfectly suited for probing flowers. Apart from some bats, the honey possum (*Tarsipes rostratus*) is the only mammal in the world that feeds exclusively on nectar and pollen. Although they are still common, the plants on which they rely for their food are threatened by the killer dieback disease.

Honey possums, also known as noolbengers, are mouse-sized, with a combined head and body length of about 70 millimetres. They have a disproportionately long pointed snout, rounded ears and a very long tail. The brownish-grey fur on the back is usually striped, with a darker central band and paler bands on either side.

These minute creatures are found only in the South-West of WA but they are common within this area. They live in heathlands which support a rich assemblage of plant species such as banksias. In hot weather, honey possums are mostly nocturnal. On the South Coast they are occasionally seen feeding on flowering banksias and eucalypts during daylight hours in the cooler months, when they may be active in the morning and late afternoon.

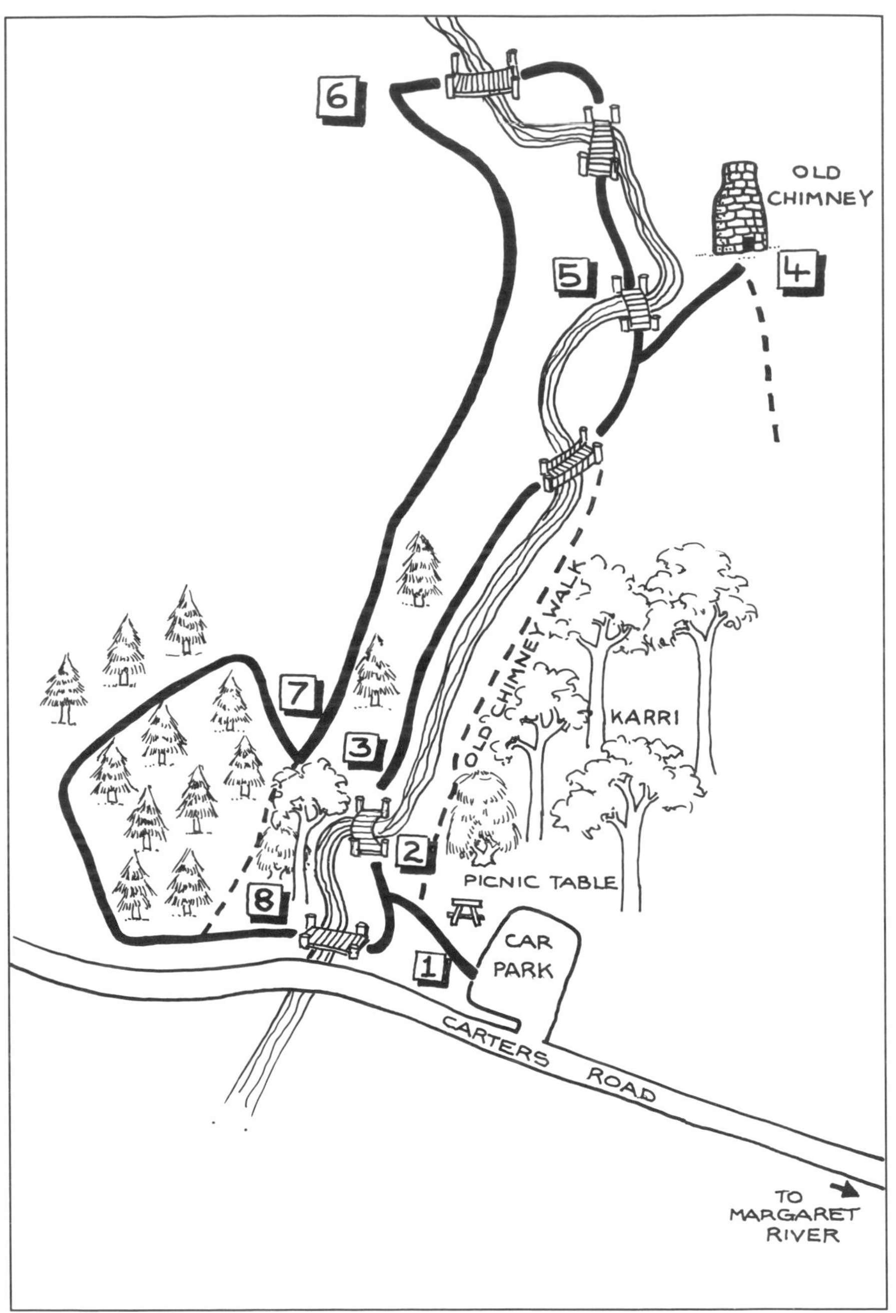
6
OLD
CHIMNEY
5
4
OLD CHIMNEY WALK
KARRI
7
3
2
PICNIC TABLE
8
CAR
PARK
1
CARTERS ROAD
TO
MARGARET
RIVER

Brook and Bridge Walk

16

Margaret River

Length: *4 km.*
Grade: *2.*
Walk time: *1 to $1^1/_2$ hours.*

This walk is a combination of three marked walks that all commence from Carters Road, just a short distance from the attractive town of Margaret River.

1. Begin from the trailhead sign on Carters Road, initially following the 'Big Brook' walk. This section of the walk, through peppermint and karri, is also part of the 'Rails to Trails' walk/cyclepath and follows an old railway embankment.
2. The first old railway bridge you negotiate is something of an engineering feat. Built in the early 1900s, it is curved from one side of the Brook to the other. The early timber bridge building pioneers built only a few similar bridges in the State. The railway line linked Busselton and Margaret River.
3. From this point, you roughly follow the course of the brook, crossing and recrossing it a number of times as you head north-east.
4. Just after crossing the second bridge, detour through the 'Old Chimney Walk'. Not long after reaching a blackboy studded clearing you will see one of the last two remaining curved brick chimneys in the State. It was once a sawdust burner for a softwood sawmill operating at the site in the 1950s.
5. Return to the path along the old railway line, taking the shortcut to your right after retracing your steps, to cross the brook three more times.
6. The path leaves the brook and soon turns sharply to the west.
7. You eventually reach an area planted with some of the State's largest radiata pines. Detour along the 'Pine Plantation Walk', which turns sharply right. The atmosphere of the walk is enhanced by mosses and lichens growing on logs that have fallen on the forest floor. In places, torn pine cones litter the path - a sign that black-cockatoos have been feeding in the plantation. They rip the cones apart with their powerful, hooked beaks to obtain the seeds.
8. After rejoining the 'Big Brook Walk', follow the signs back to the starting point, crossing a small wooden bridge en route.

Where is it? *About 2 km from Margaret River.*
Travelling time: *5 minutes from Margaret River.*
Facilities: *Picnic tables, car park.*
Best season: *All year.*

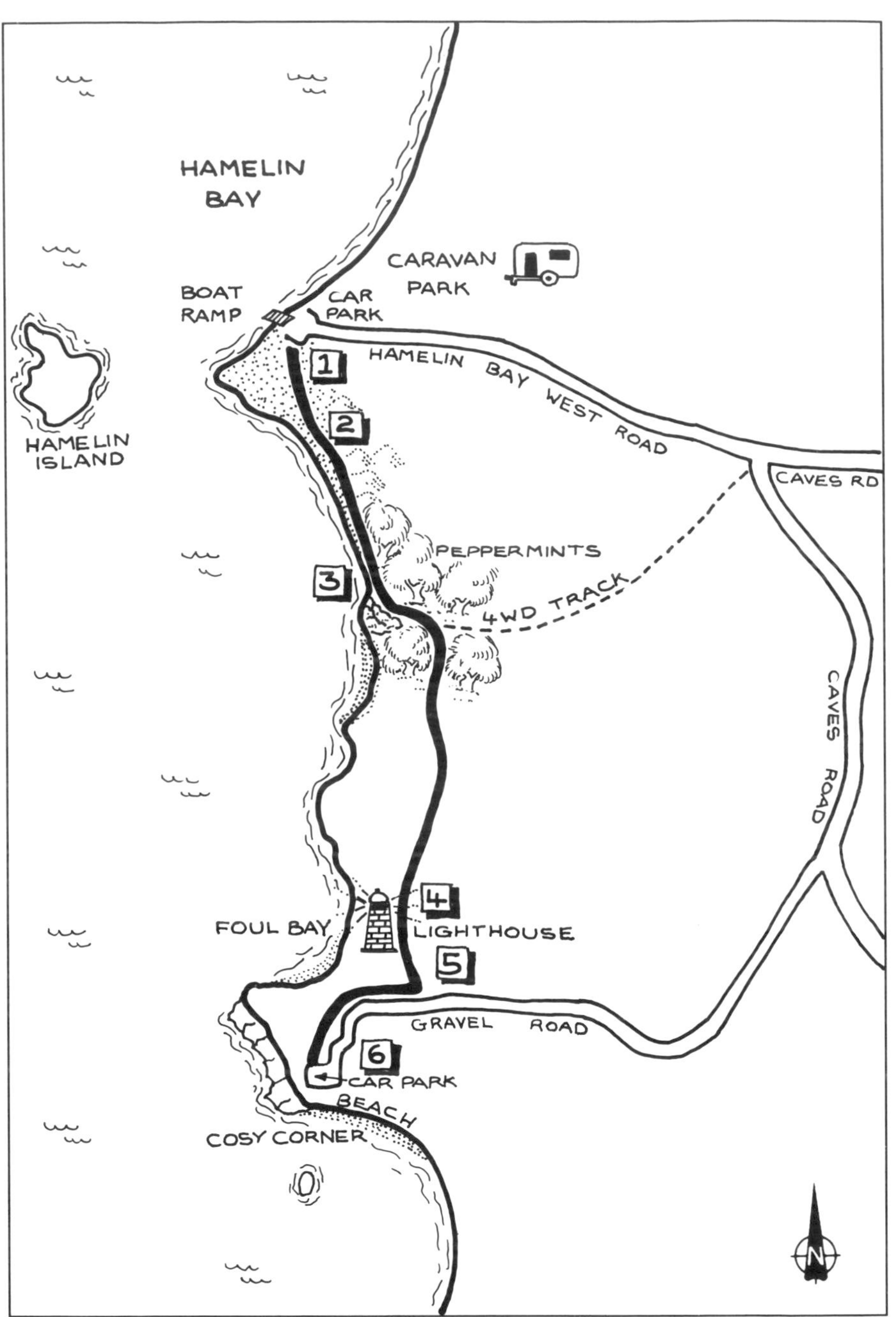
HAMELIN BAY
CARAVAN PARK
BOAT RAMP
CAR PARK
HAMELIN ISLAND
1
HAMELIN BAY WEST ROAD
2
CAVES RD
PEPPERMINTS
3
4WD TRACK
CAVES ROAD
4
FOUL BAY
LIGHTHOUSE
5
GRAVEL ROAD
6
CAR PARK
BEACH
COSY CORNER
N

Hamelin Bay to Cosy Corner

17

Leeuwin-Naturaliste National Park

Length: *6.5 km.*
Grade: *4.*
Walk time: *2 hours.*

This excellent half day walk has magnificent views. It involves some easy scrambling and negotiating short, steep sections. Organise a car to meet you, or return along the beach to complete a 13 kilometre circuit. The trail is part of the 140-kilometre Cape to Cape Walk Track. A brochure for Section 5 (with a total length of 29 kilometres) is available from local CALM offices and tourist outlets for a nominal fee.

1. Begin at the boat ramp in Hamelin Bay. Named after Captain J F E Hamelin, commander of the French corvette *Naturaliste*, Hamelin Bay was a thriving port and community during the timber era of the 1890s. The jetty was built in 1882 and extended in 1898. The dangers of its position, exposed to the north-west winds, are evident from the 11 wrecks which lie around its shores. Three barques, *Nor'wester, Lovespring* and *Katinka*, were wrecked in a single night with the loss of five lives during a particularly violent storm on July 22, 1900. Today Hamelin Bay is a popular swimming and fishing beach with a caravan park where the timber yards once stood. Watch for stingrays, which often swim close to shore underneath the remains of the jetty.
2. From the boat ramp, the track crosses the bare headland then follows the beach for one kilometre. Do not walk near the edge, as cliffs in this area can be fragile.
3. Just before a rocky limestone outcrop, look for the markers and steps heading off the beach. Pick up a four-wheel-drive track which leads through peppermint (*Agonis flexuosa*) woodlands inland for half a kilometre. Take care not to miss the turn-off, which heads south to climb up to the Foul Bay lighthouse.
4. The lighthouse is 3.9 metres high and is fully operational. From this vantage point, there are superb views back to Hamelin Island, where the original lighthouse was established in 1937. It was powered by acetylene, hauled across in cylinders via an aerial cableway, and the remains of the brick structure and gantry can still be seen on the island. In 1967 the light was moved to this much higher position, 80 metres above sea level.
5. The trail reaches the Cosy Corner Road, following it to the Cosy Corner car park.
6. Cosy Corner is known for its white sandy beach, red granite headlands and offshore islands of limestone. A sanctuary for thousands of seabirds, the islands

are remnants from a period when the sea level was much lower and the dunes extended far out into the bay. They are also surrounded by stunning reefs and drop-offs that are home to a myriad of colourful marine animals, such as giant blue gropers, harlequin fish, and curious cuttlefish.

Where is it? *19 km from Augusta and 309 km from Perth.*
Travelling time: *15 minutes from Augusta.*
Facilities: *Toilets, boat ramp, commercial caravan park.*
Best season: *All year during good weather.*

Neil Taylor

CHRISTMAS SPIDER

Christmas or jewel spiders (*Gasteracantha minax*) live in home gardens and scrub all over southern Australia. They produce beautiful large orb webs. At times and in places where there is an abundance of very small insects, hundreds of webs may swathe surrounding bush.

You can easily recognise the small, black spiny spider by its star-shaped abdomen, with bright yellow or white raised patches on a black background. Occasionally there are colour variations: all black, red and white body patches, orange and black legs, or greenish black legs. The six, tapering spines, which give the spider its star shape, are longer on the female than the male, and like most spiders, the female (about 10 millimetres long) is larger than the male (about three millimetres long). Male Christmas spiders have an important mating ritual. Because of their smaller size, they must communicate their intention, or be mistaken by the female for prey and killed. Part of a male jewel spider's courtship ritual is to pluck a successful message on the female's web with his front legs. This stimulates her interest and suppresses her predatory impulse.

In early summer the spiders mature and are quite obvious on their webs. During summer the mature spiders mate. By autumn, most of the spiders have laid their eggs in a fluffy, silken yellow sac near the web. Shortly afterwards they die. The spiderlings hatch during winter, but it is not until mid-spring that they or their webs are large enough to attract attention once more.

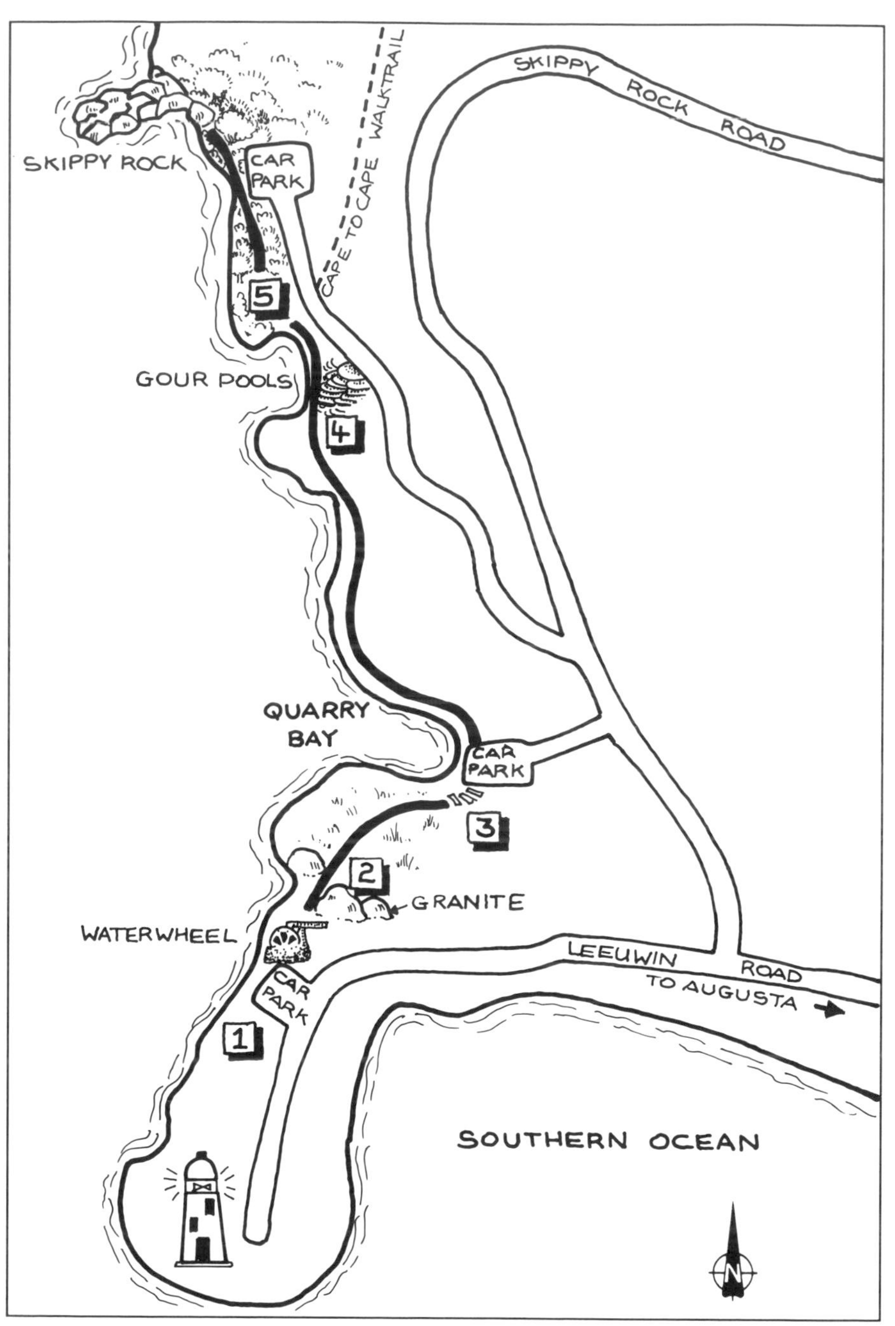
SKIPPY ROCK ROAD
CAPE TO CAPE WALKTRAIL
SKIPPY ROCK
CAR PARK
5
GOUR POOLS
4
QUARRY BAY
CAR PARK
3
2
GRANITE
WATERWHEEL
LEEUWIN ROAD
TO AUGUSTA
CAR PARK
1
SOUTHERN OCEAN
N

Water Wheel to Skippy Rock

18

Leeuwin-Naturaliste National Park

Length: *3 km.*
Grade: *2.*
Walk time: *1 hour.*

This short, but varied walk takes in beach, rocks and bush. It is part of the 140-kilometre Cape to Cape Walk Track. A brochure for Section 5 (with a total length of 29 kilometres) is available from local CALM offices and tourist outlets for a nominal fee. The grades are easy. You can combine this walk with a visit to the Cape Leeuwin Lighthouse, which though still in use is open for daily tours.

1. Begin at the Leeuwin Waterwheel, near the Cape Leeuwin Lighthouse in Augusta. It was built to power a hydraulic ram, which would pump water from the nearby swamp to supply the lighthouse (built by Maurice Coleman Davies in 1896) and keepers' cottages. It quickly became encrusted with a coating of limestone and is now frozen in rock.
2. Head north over some massive granite domes, through low grass and heath at the south end of Quarry Bay.
3. Before climbing the steps to the car park, take a look at the south end of the Bay. Here, limestone was hewn for the blocks used to build the Cape Leeuwin lighthouse. The many small chips of stone which can be found at the base of the cliff, residue from this quarrying activity, are already well cemented together after only 100 years.
4. Continue in a north-easterly direction. The path follows flat granite rocks, where you may be able to see sooty oystercatchers foraging for shellfish. Numerous seepages from beneath the limestone have built up tiers of beautiful rimstone, or 'gour' pools which spill out onto the granite. Late winter to spring is a good time to explore here, when there is plenty of running water. However, be careful of slippery rocks.
5. After reaching a small, shelly beach, the path heads up through dense coastal vegetation to the road into Skippy Rock. Try to identify the different plants. Native rosemary (*Olearia axillaris*) has a pleasant herbal smell when you crush its leaves. Thick-leaved fanflower (*Scaevola crassifolia*), has broad, thick and slightly fleshy leaves up to eight centimetres long and small pale blue to violet fan-like flowers. You can also see coastal banjine (*Pimelea ferruginea*), with domed pink flower heads, basket bush (*Spyridium globulosum*), coastal sword sedge (*Lepidosperma gladiatum*) and Australian bluebell (*Sollya heterophylla*),

with its small mauve to blue, bell-like flowers, while dodder laurel clambers over neighbouring plants. There is a pleasant rest area in a grove of shady peppermint (*Agonis flexuosa*) trees. After reaching Skippy Rock, you can either retrace your steps or ask someone to pick you up.

Where is it? *The walk begins at Cape Leeuwin, in Augusta.*
Travelling time: *5 minutes from the town centre.*
Facilities: *Car parks, water.*
Best season: *Late winter to spring, when there is a lot of running water.*

Neil Taylor

The Karri Forest Walks 19 - 36

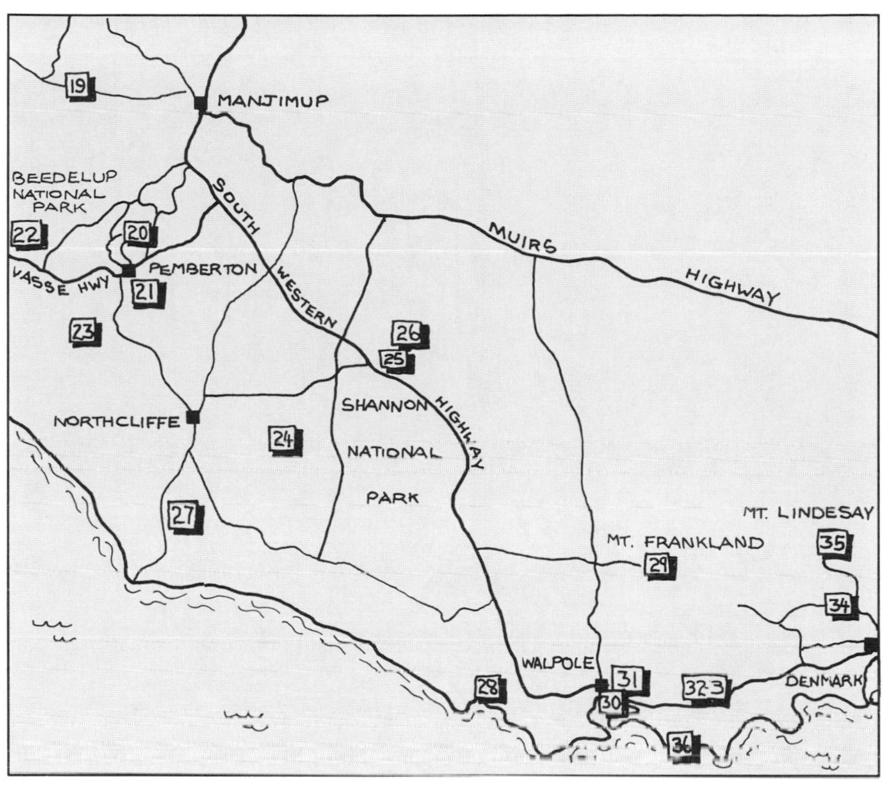

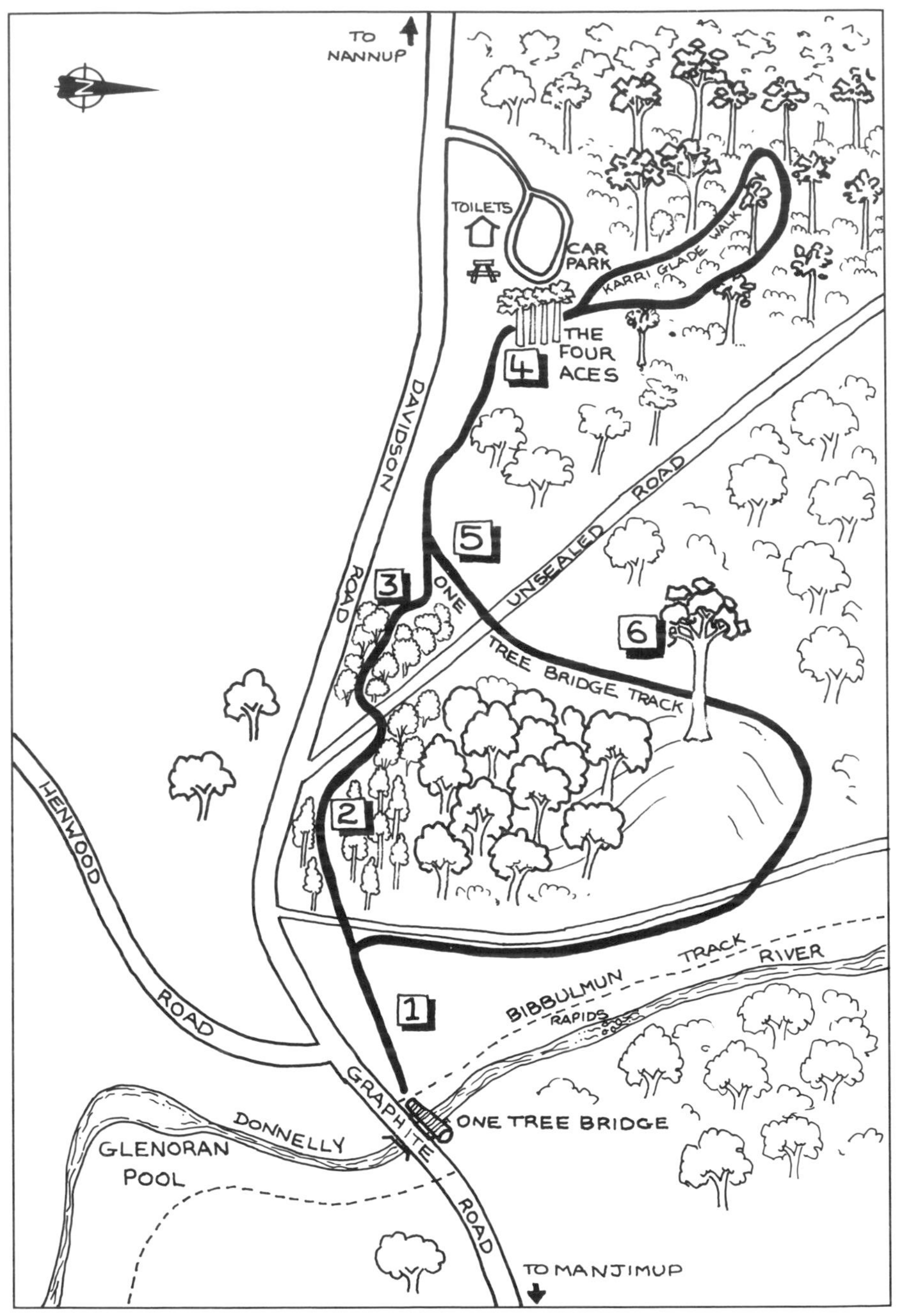
TO NANNUP
TOILETS
CAR PARK
KARRI GLADE WALK
THE FOUR ACES
4
DAVIDSON ROAD
5
3
ONE TREE BRIDGE TRACK
UNSEALED ROAD
6
HENWOOD ROAD
2
1
BIBBULMUN TRACK
RIVER
RAPIDS
GRAPHITE ROAD
ONE TREE BRIDGE
DONNELLY
GLENORAN POOL
TO MANJIMUP

One Tree Bridge Loop

19

One Tree Bridge Conservation Park

Length: *2 km.*
Grade: *1.*
Walk time: *40 minutes.*

This scenic walk allows you to explore One Tree Bridge, the Four Aces and the towering forests in between. The northern part of the loop track is steep as it descends into the Donnelly Valley.

1. Begin at the One Tree Bridge. This was built by felling one immense karri tree over the Donnelly River.
2. Continue along the track (passing by the turn-off to your right) until you reach a grove of young karri trees. They are locked in battle for light and nutrients and only the taller, stronger plants thrive.
3. Crossing an unsealed road, continue until you reach an area densely vegetated with the lush understorey plants karri hazel (*Trymalium floribundum*) and water bush (*Bossiaea aquifolium*). Karri hazel is also known as soapbush. When the leaves are used to scrub the hands they produce a froth similar to soap. Nyoongar men used a quartz knife to skin kangaroos and to cut the meat, which often resulted in numerous cuts on their hands. Soapbush was used to wash away the blood. Red gum, known as kino, from the marri (*Corymbia calophylla*) tree may have also been applied to any cuts to prevent infections.
4. Continue ahead, ignoring another turn-off to the right, until you reach Four Aces, four giant karri trees in a straight line. You may choose to continue along the Four Aces Karri Glade Walk, a 700-metre loop that wends through some of the tallest trees in the district.
5. Retrace your steps to the turn-off and head to the left up the One Tree Bridge Track. This takes you on a loop through mixed jarrah, marri and blackbutt forest.
6. You will pass a big karri on the hill top. The grade of the track is quite steep. From here, return to the original trail and back to One Tree Bridge.

Where is it? *22 km west of Manjimup on Graphite Road.*
Travelling time: *20 minutes from Manjimup.*
Facilities: *Toilets, barbecues, picnic shelters, information and car parking.*
Best season: *All year.*

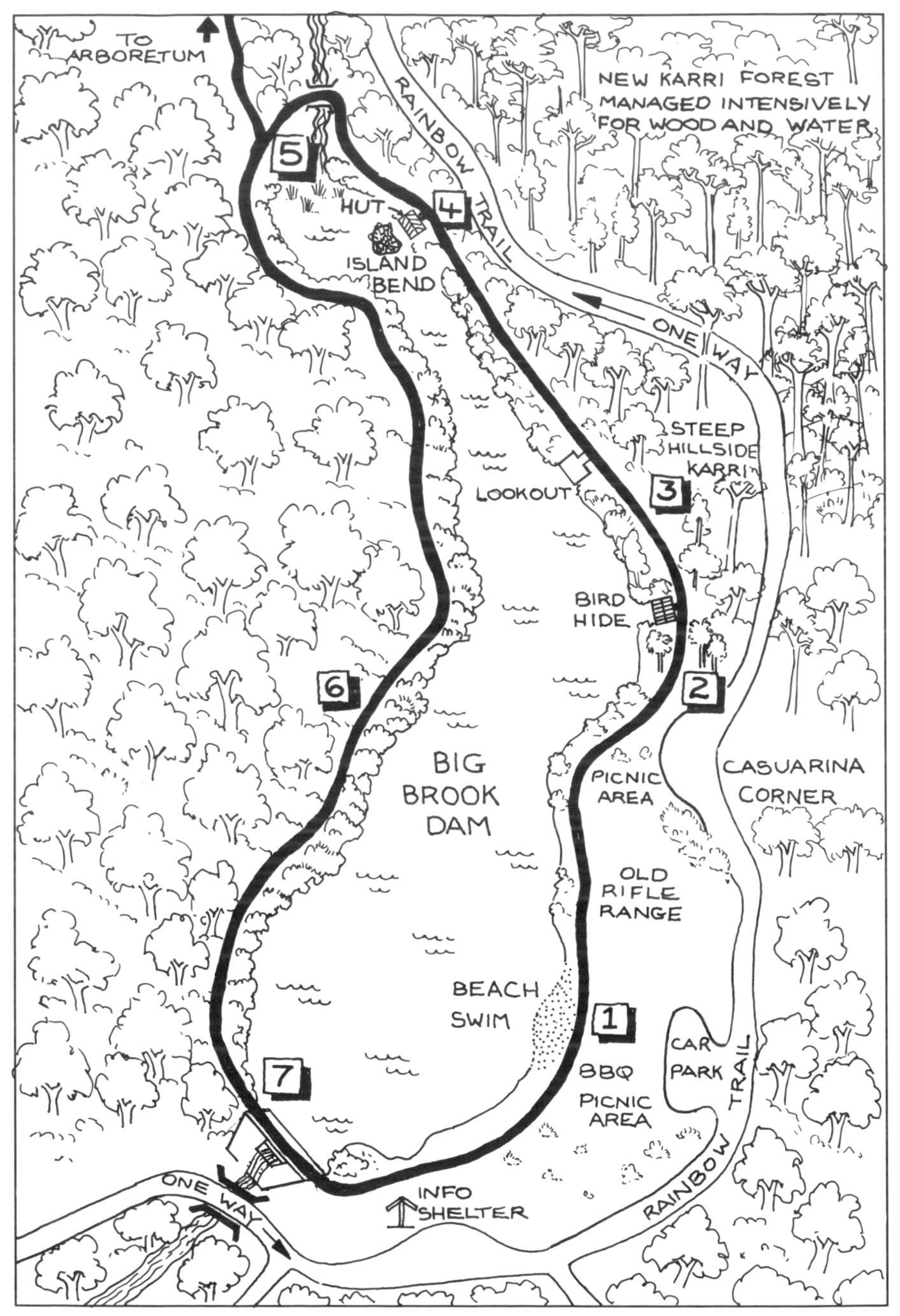
TO ARBORETUM
NEW KARRI FOREST
MANAGED INTENSIVELY
FOR WOOD AND WATER
RAINBOW TRAIL
5
HUT
4
ISLAND
BEND
ONE WAY
STEEP
HILLSIDE
KARRI
LOOKOUT
3
BIRD
HIDE
2
6
BIG
BROOK
DAM
PICNIC
AREA
CASUARINA
CORNER
OLD
RIFLE
RANGE
BEACH
SWIM
1
CAR
PARK
7
BBQ
PICNIC
AREA
TRAIL
RAINBOW
ONE WAY
INFO
SHELTER

Big Brook Dam

Pemberton

Length: *4 km.*
Grade: *2.*
Walk time: *1 to 1½ hours.*

Big Brook Dam was built in 1986 to supplement water supplies to Pemberton and the nearby trout hatchery. A walktrail loops around the dam, passing through the Big Brook forest. It is accessible to wheelchairs, prams and strollers and has shelters and seats at rest points along the way.

1. Head in a westerly direction from the picnic area near the car park. A small sandy beach lines the shore.
2. As you walk along the trail through regrowth forest, keep an eye open for waterfowl on the dam and many other forest birds, such as lorikeets, ringneck parrots and grey fantails. Try to identify the Warren River cedar (*Agonis juniperina*). Belonging to the myrtle family, this tree grows in valleys or along watercourses and creeks. It is usually about 15 metres tall, with a straight trunk and tufts and clumps of leaves. It produces white flowers in May. Aboriginal people called this tree "wattie" and used it to make spear shafts. There is a bird hide along the dam edge.
3. To your right is a steep hillside densely forested with regrowth karri. Between 1920 and 1928 the entire area around Big Brook was clearfelled, and the enormous logs were hauled to the sawmill at Pemberton by steam locomotive. In 1930, a spark from a steam locomotive started a wildfire, which swept down the valley, burning farms and nearly reaching Pemberton township. The fire resulted in dense karri regeneration and regrowth, and today the magnificent karri trees are more than 65 years old and 50-60 metres high. A lookout gives good views over the dam.
4. A hut overlooks a small, densely vegetated island.
5. Cross Big Brook on a log bridge. The turn-off to the Big Brook Arboretum is just after the crossing. Many different trees from around the world, including the American redwood, were planted here by foresters in 1929 so they could study their growth in the Pemberton area. You may choose to add the extra 1.2 kilometres onto your walk, otherwise continue around the dam to another wooden hut, with entertaining information panels around the walls. This is a good rest area.
6. On the southern side of Big Brook, the walktrail follows part of an old tramway

used to transport karri logs from the forest. This section of trail is densely vegetated and the dam is obscured.

7. The path leads over the dam wall to the other side of Big Brook and from here it is only a short distance back to the car park.

Where is it? *Drive north-east from Pemberton along the Golf Links Road and follow the signs to Big Brook Dam, about 10 km from Pemberton.*
Travelling time: *10 minutes from Pemberton.*
Facilities: *Barbecues, picnic tables, toilets.*
Best season: *All year.*

Tammie Reid

GOLDEN WHISTLER

The golden whistler (*Pachycephala pectoralis*) is a typical bird of the South-West forests. The birds glean most of their prey from trees, but sometimes swoop out to take insects on the wing or to rifle through the litter on the forest floor. Their loud whistling *chee-chee-chee-chee-tu-whit* rings out noisily throughout the breeding season.

Golden whistlers are common in south-western Australia, from Shark Bay to Esperance. They are also found in parts of eastern Australia. They seem to prefer taller, wetter coastal forests but they are also found in eucalypt woodland, heath and mallee areas. Only mature male birds have brightly coloured plumage. They have a black head, face and beak with a white throat. The back of the head and chest are a bright yellow, the tail and wing feathers are dusky black to grey and the back is a yellowish-green. The females are a dull greyish-green.

The birds generally eat insects and their larvae, which they sometimes supplement with berries. Their nest is untidy and shaped like a cup. They lay two eggs between September and January and both parents incubate the eggs and care for their young.

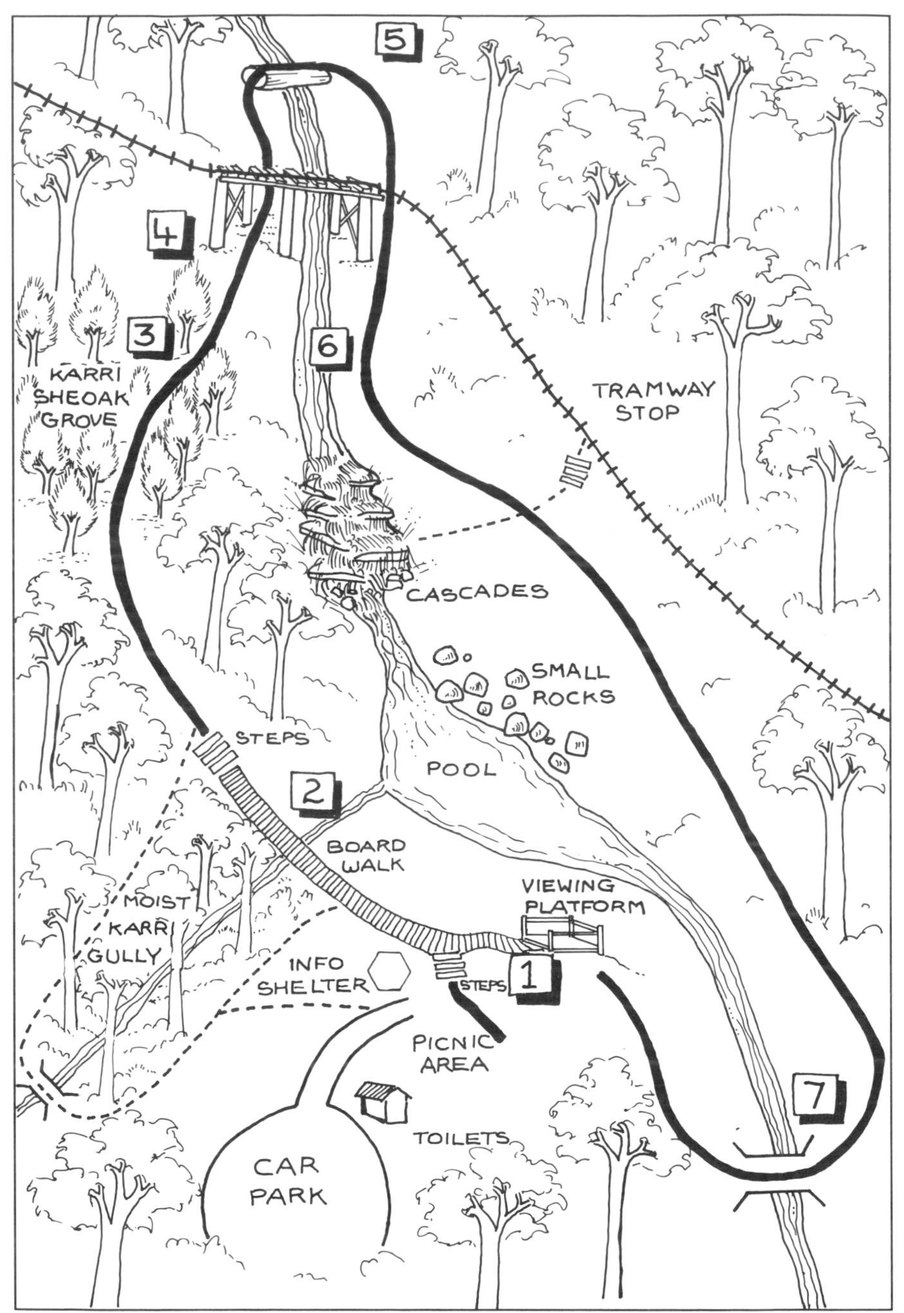
5
4
3
KARRI
SHEOAK
GROVE
6
TRAMWAY
STOP
CASCADES
SMALL
ROCKS
STEPS
POOL
2
BOARD
WALK
VIEWING
PLATFORM
MOIST
KARRI
GULLY
INFO
SHELTER
STEPS
1
PICNIC
AREA
7
TOILETS
CAR
PARK

The Cascades

Gloucester National Park ($)

21

Length: *1.2 km.*
Grade: *1.*
Walk time: *30-40 minutes.*

These rocky rapids, set amidst the karri forest at the southern end of Gloucester National Park, provide a place for an outdoor lunch, a leisurely afternoon stroll, or a few peaceful hours of fly fishing.

1. You obtain your first view of the Cascades from the viewing platform near the parking area. The Lefroy Brook tumbles over a series of rocky shelves, which vary from a gentle flow in midsummer to a raging torrent in winter.
2. Heading in a north-easterly direction, step down to the boardwalk that crosses a tributary of the Lefroy Brook. The stream is in a moist gully that supports karri and its typical understorey plants.
3. A little further on, you pass through groves of karri sheoak (*Allocasuarina decussata*). This tree is almost entirely confined to the karri forests. It grows up to 15 metres high and has thick, corky bark with vertical fissures. Its "needles" are actually slender, jointed branchlets.
4. The trail passes under the Northcliffe tramway, once used to transport karri logs across the Lefroy Brook. It is now used by sightseers to tour the karri forest between Northcliffe and Pemberton.
5. A bridge further upstream, made from one long karri log, takes you over the brook. Near the water you'll see some lush fern and reed growth.
6. Crossing over the tramway, this time on the other side of the brook, you will pass along the eastern side of the Cascades, which tumbles into a pool, surrounded with small rocks.
7. Continue along the walktrail to cross another bridge and return to the viewing platform.

Where is it? *6 km south of Pemberton. Head towards Northcliffe and turn left at Glauders Road. Follow the signs to the Cascades.*
Travelling time: *10 minutes from Pemberton.*
Facilities: *Toilets, barbecues, picnic tables, information and car parking.*
Best season: *All year.*

Tammie Reid

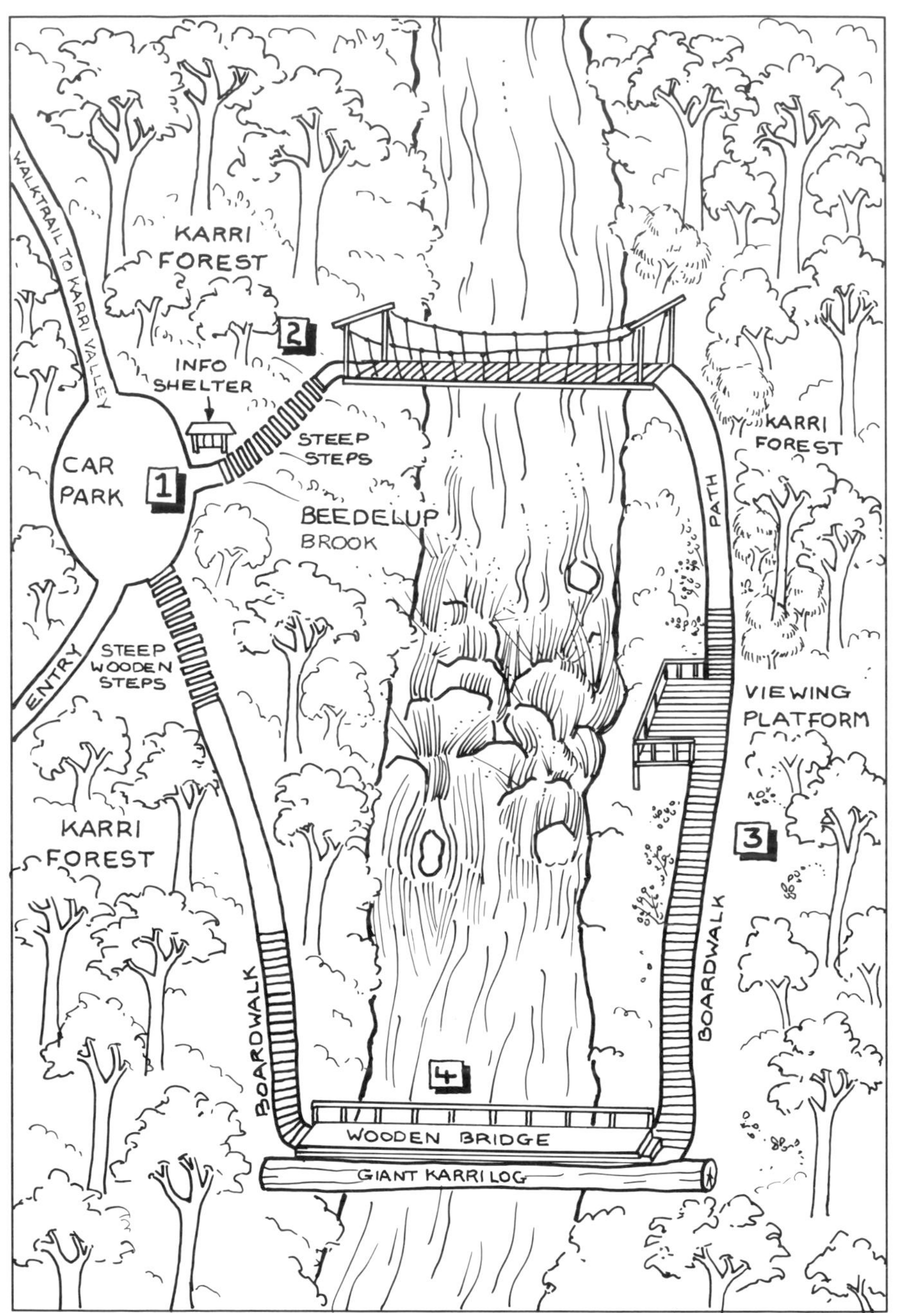
WALKTRAIL TO KARRI VALLEY
KARRI FOREST
2
INFO SHELTER
CAR PARK
1
STEEP STEPS
BEEDELUP BROOK
ENTRY
STEEP WOODEN STEPS
KARRI FOREST
KARRI FOREST
PATH
VIEWING PLATFORM
3
BOARDWALK
BOARDWALK
4
WOODEN BRIDGE
GIANT KARRI LOG

Beedelup Falls

22

Beedelup National Park ($)

Length: *300 m.*
Grade: *2.*
Walk time: *20 minutes at a very leisurely pace.*

This short but extremely scenic walk should not be missed by visitors to Pemberton. The falls are the major attraction of Beedelup National Park, and are in full flow during winter and spring. The falls can be viewed along a walktrail and from two bridges and a lookout. Fees must be paid to enter the park.

1. The walk loop starts at the car park. Descend the steep wooden steps through a corridor of trees and creepers to reach the first bridge of the falls.
2. There is an excellent view of the falls, which cascade for 100 metres over a series of steep granite rocks, from a suspension bridge which crosses Beedelup Brook. In winter, when the falls are rapid, you may be able to feel the spray. Beedelup National Park was named after Beedelup Brook, which has been shown on plans since 1875. It is an Aboriginal name said to mean "place of water".
3. Walk upstream along a boardwalk, looking for the masses of maidenhair fern and moss which creep up the base of trees. The understorey is lush, and the atmosphere damp and often misty, because of the abundance of water. There are many peppermints (*Agonis flexuosa*) and swamp peppermints (*Agonis linearifolia*), recognised by their similar clusters of white flowers, but smaller and more rigid leaves. The lemon-scented darwinia (*Darwinia citriodora*), a sprawling shrub with leaves held in opposite pairs, which have a lemony smell when crushed, is also common on the walktrail. Karri hazel, chorilaena, hibbertia and tassel bush mix with water bush and the myrtle wattle (*Acacia myrtifolia*), which is smaller and has paler yellow flowers than the karri wattle.
4. Pass over a second bridge then traverse a section of boardwalk and path before climbing more wooden stairs to return to the car park.

Where is it? *The park is adjacent to Karri Valley Resort, on the Vasse Highway 17 km west of Pemberton.*
Travelling time: *15 minutes from Pemberton.*
Facilities: *Car park, boardwalk, lookouts.*
Best season: *Winter and spring, when the falls are in full flow.*

Judy Wheeler and Tammie Reid

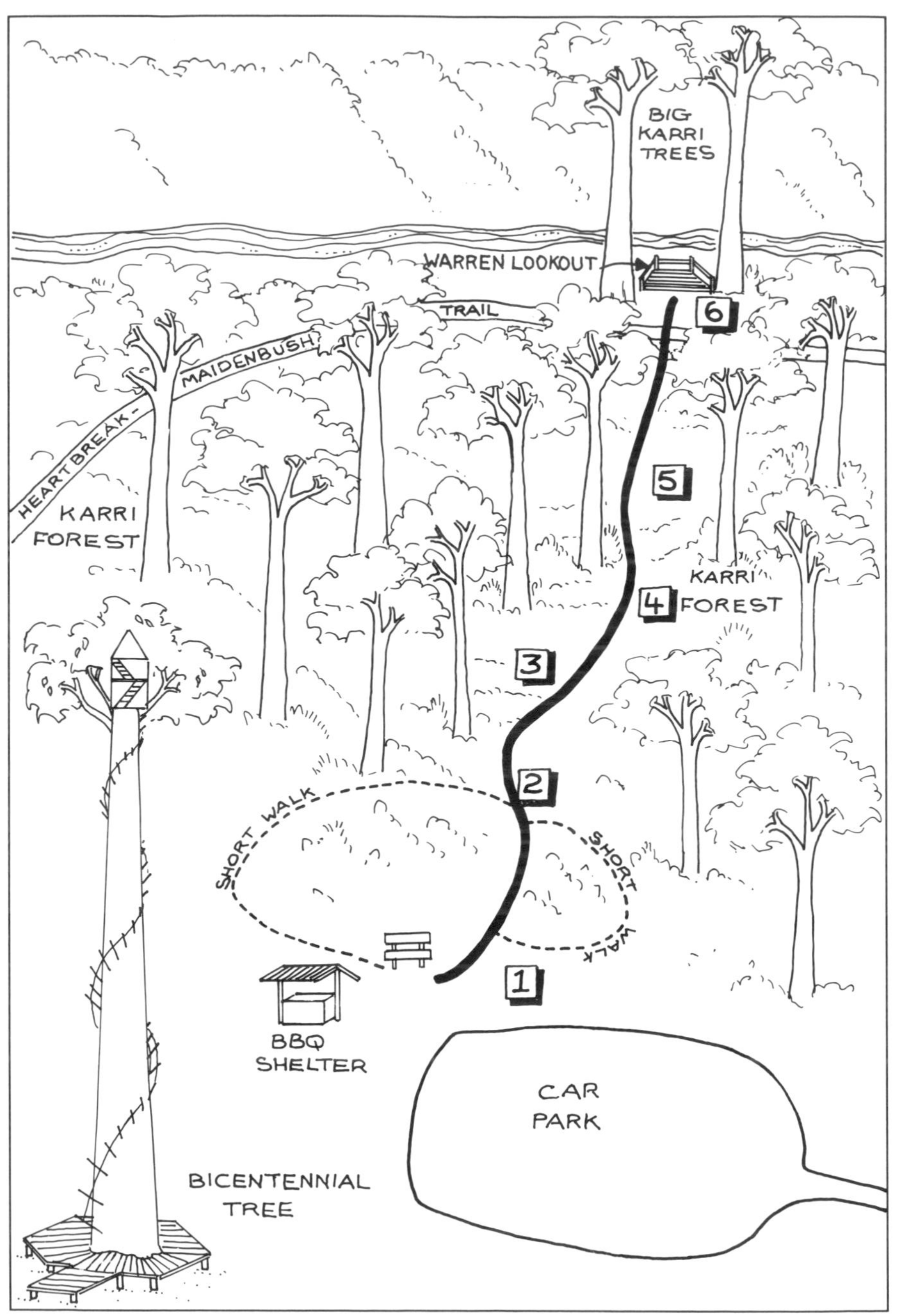
BIG
KARRI
TREES
WARREN LOOKOUT
TRAIL
MAIDENBUSH
HEARTBREAK-
KARRI
FOREST
6
5
KARRI
4 FOREST
3
2
SHORT WALK
SHORT
WALK
1
BBQ
SHELTER
CAR
PARK
BICENTENNIAL
TREE

Bicentennial Tree to Warren Lookout

23

Warren National Park ($)

Length: *2.4 km return.*
Grade: *2.*
Walk time: *Allow 1 hour.*

If you want to experience some huge old growth karri forest, and the best of the Warren River Valley, take this walk in Warren National Park. You can begin from either end of the walk: the Bicentennial Tree (well signposted just off Old Vasse Road) or Warren Lookout, found on Heartbreak Trail. The trail is well marked and at either end of the journey there is a treat in store!

1. Start from Bicentennial Tree and find the trailhead sign adjacent to the covered barbecue area. Here you will find a brief description of the walk and the trail markers to follow. You can explore the site before you begin and visit the interpretive shelter which contains information about fire lookout trees and the local area. Bicentennial Tree was pegged as a fire lookout tree in 1988. You can climb almost 70 metres to the top to take in great views of the karri forest and surrounding countryside. Be warned - this climb is not for the faint hearted!
2. From the trailhead you will begin to descend into the Warren River Valley. When the karri is in flower (which can be from September to February) the purple-crowned lorikeets can be deafening, as they dart around feeding on the flowers high up in the tree tops.
3. Still heading downhill (remember you have to come back uphill later) stop along the way and take in the smell of the karri forest - a mixture of sweet, musty, damp, earthy aromas.
4. In winter, the kingdom of the karri also becomes the kingdom of the fungi. Fungi of every imaginable shape and colour pop up through the damp ground, or begin to grow on rotting debris on the forest floor. Try to see how many different types of fungi you can find. Coral fungi is particularly attractive - but very fragile.
5. Along the walk there are many huge trees quite close to the track. The age of the forest here is probably between 200 and 300 years old. Look up and into the forest - see how widely spaced the trees are here. Young karri forests are much more tightly packed, with many more trees per hectare. As the forest ages, the stronger and healthier trees take over and, in the competition for light, space and nutrients, many trees die. The big trees that remain today are in the later stages of their lives.

6. Time for a breather. Stop and take in the view from the Warren Lookout. The ground falls away from you and you can look down to the meandering river, which is often hung with mist, framed between the karri. Warren River was discovered by Lieutenant Preston in 1831 and the name was probably applied to it by Governor Stirling, possibly in honour of a friend of his, Captain Warren. At the lookout there is information about the river and its catchment. Turn around and head back the same way to Bicentennial Tree, which is also a good place to stop for lunch.

Where is it? *Warren National Park lies 15 km south-west of Pemberton on the Old Vasse Road.*
Travelling time: *10 minutes from Pemberton.*
Facilities: *Covered picnic and barbecue area, free gas and wood barbecues, toilets, information, water.*
Best season: *All year.*

Rod Annear

RED-TAILED BLACK-COCKATOO

Red-tailed black-cockatoos (*Calyptorhynchus banksii*) are large, spectacular and noisy birds. However, in the tall jarrah and karri forests they usually stay high up in the canopy, where they feast on marri and other eucalypt seeds. They also form smaller groups than in other areas, usually pairs or small family parties.

Male cockatoos are uniformly black, with a brilliant crimson band on the tail feathers. The females are brownish-black, with yellow speckles and light yellow to orange tail bands. Adult birds are between 50 and 61 centimetres long.

While they are not considered endangered, red-tailed black-cockatoos are given special protection under the Wildlife Conservation Act. Their nests are often robbed by illegal wildlife traffickers and their habitat has been considerably reduced by clearing. They require nesting hollows with an entrance at least 180 millimetres wide. In the karri forest these can be 30 metres from the ground.

Red-tailed black-cockatoos lay a single egg in their nesting hollow, which they enter tail first. The male feeds his partner while she sits on the eggs and broods the nestlings. These seed-eating birds extract the nutritious seeds of marri by tearing open the base of the fruits. Their call is a harsh *kree*.

FARMS
BOORARA ROAD
BOORARA LOOKOUT
TREE NO LONGER IN USE
1
PICNIC AREA
2
TRAIL FOLLOWS OLD FOREST ROAD HERE
3
STEEP NARROW PATH
SMALL ROCK OUTCROPS
GOOD VIEWS ACROSS THE CANTERBURY VALLEY
4
LANE POOLE FALLS

Boorara Tree

24

Lane-Poole Falls

Length: *5 km.*
Grade: *2.*
Walk time: *$1^1/_2$ hours.*

Follow the signs off Boorara Road to the tree which, until 1977, was a fire lookout tower. This marks the start of the track to the misty veil of Lane Poole Falls.

1. Begin at the Boorara Lookout. The cabin and top section of the tree was once perched high up in a karri. It has now been cut off, lowered to the ground and set up at the foot of the tree. In this position, it gives visitors a chance to examine the old techniques of tower construction at close quarters. It was removed because the tree and cabin had become unsafe. The lookout was built in 1952 by legendary axeman George Reynolds, who also pegged the ladder and lopped the branches of the Gloucester Tree near Pemberton. He never used a safety belt and would lean into the wind when cutting off limbs at a great height.
2. Follow the old firebreak through the karri trees. Creepers scramble across the dense forest floor, and in spring they contribute to the colourful wildflower display. At such times, you can usually see the orange, pink and yellow pea flowers of coral vine (*Kennedia coccinea*), the purple pea flowers of native wisteria (*Hardenbergia comptoniana*) and white clematis (*Clematis pubescens*) intermixing with the yellow wattle, prickly moses (*Acacia pulchella*).
3. As you near the falls, the track narrows and descends steeply.
4. The Lane Poole Falls is on the Canterbury River. During winter, water tumbles over a granite wall to a pool 12 metres below. In summer, the flow may be reduced to a trickle, but you can still enjoy the atmosphere of this hidden valley with its towering river banksias (*Banksia seminuda*). This attractive, erect tree is one of the taller banksia species, growing up to 20 metres high with a straight trunk and hard, fissured grey bark. In late summer to late winter it produces yellow, cylindrical flower-spikes.

Where is it? *About 18 km south-east of Northcliffe.*
Travelling time: *15 minutes from Northcliffe.*
Facilities: *Picnic site.*
Best season: *Winter for the falls and spring for the wildflowers.*

Tammie Reid

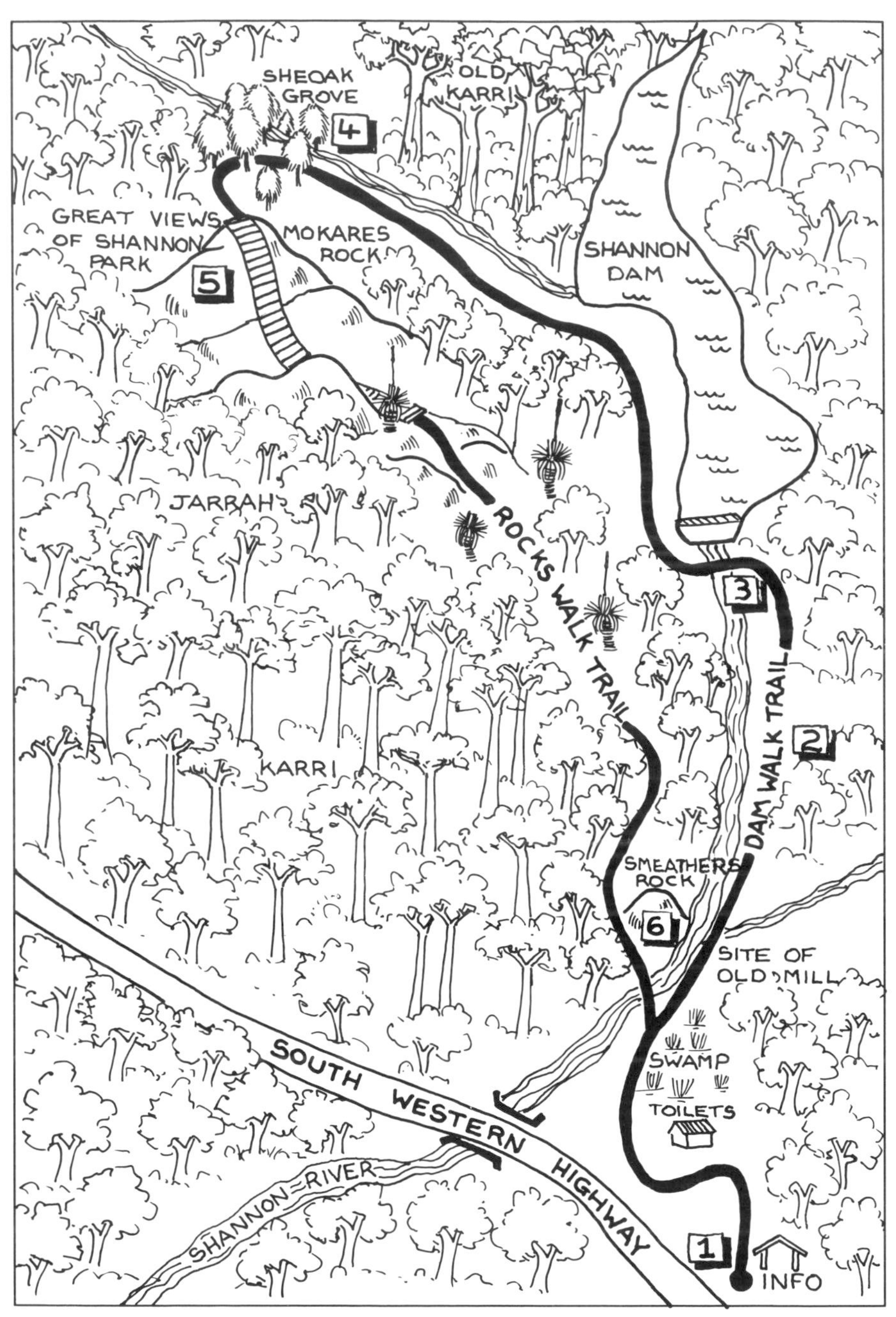

SHEOAK GROVE
4
OLD KARRI
SHANNON DAM
GREAT VIEWS OF SHANNON PARK
5
MOKARES ROCK
JARRAH
ROCKS WALK TRAIL
3
DAM WALK TRAIL
2
KARRI
SMEATHERS ROCK
6
SITE OF OLD MILL
SWAMP
TOILETS
SOUTH WESTERN HIGHWAY
SHANNON RIVER
1
INFO

The Rocks Walktrail

25

Shannon National Park

Length: *5.5 km.*
Grade: *2.*
Walk time: *2 hours.*

The walktrail leads to peaceful Shannon Dam and Mokare's Rock, one of many granite domes found in the karri forest.

1. Begin at the information shelter. This was once the site of Shannon Mill. The town was across the highway where the camping area now stands. The first 600 metres of the trail is sealed and suitable for prams and wheelchairs.
2. Walk along the river to the dam. Like many of WA's southern rivers, the Shannon only flows after winter rains. In the dry season, the river retreats to a series of pools in a dry bed. The surrounding forest of karri was cut during the 1950s, when there was an acute shortage of timber after World War II. It has now regenerated. Remnants of an old railway line can be seen along the trail. Temporary spur lines were built to link the areas where timber was being cut to the mill.
3. From Shannon Dam, you can either return to the beginning (a 3.5 kilometre return trip) or continue to Mokare's Rock and complete the 5.5 kilometre circuit.
4. The route to Mokare's Rock is steep in places, but the view of leafy karri crowns and across the Shannon Basin is magnificent.
5. A boardwalk across Mokare's Rock protects the fragile carpet of mosses, flowers and lichens growing on the rock. It is named after an Aboriginal guide who worked for Surgeon Alexander Collie, who explored much of the land surrounding Albany.
6. Continue along the path to Smeathers Rock. From here, high above the leafy karri crowns, you gain a bird's eye view of the forest and back across the river to the old Shannon townsite. After admiring the view you pass the turn-off to the Dam to return to the starting point.

Where is it? *The park is 53 km south-east of Manjimup.*
Travelling time: *45 minutes from Manjimup and Walpole and 30 minutes from Pemberton.*
Facilities: *Barbecues, picnic tables, toilets and information.*
Best season: *October to December for forest wildflowers.*

Tammie Reid

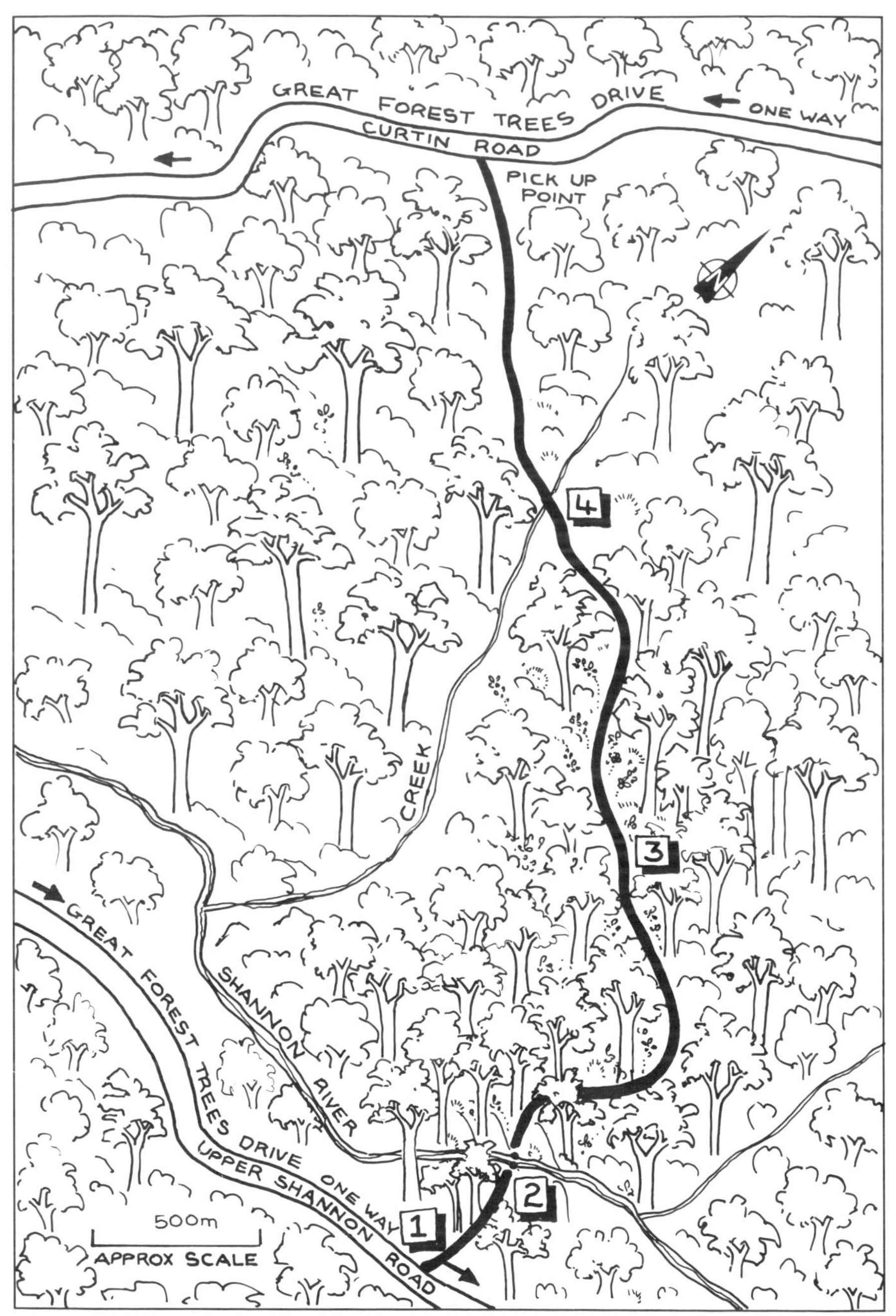
GREAT FOREST TREES DRIVE
ONE WAY
CURTIN ROAD
PICK UP POINT
N
4
CREEK
3
GREAT FOREST TREES DRIVE
ONE WAY
SHANNON RIVER
UPPER SHANNON ROAD
2
1
500m
APPROX SCALE

Great Forest Trees Walk

26

Shannon National Park

Length: *8 km return, 4 km one way.*
Grade: *3.*
Walk time: *Allow 3 hours return.*

This walk connects the arms of the one way (23 kilometre) northern loop of the scenic Great Forest Trees Drive (see page 95). The roads on the drive are not sealed but are in good condition, suitable for conventional vehicles. The walk follows an old forestry track and is steep in places, particularly where the trail crosses the Shannon River. In winter, the Shannon may burst its banks, and sometimes cut the track. If you are not feeling up to tackling the eight kilometres, you could get someone to pick you up from the other end of the trail, where it meets Curtin Road.

1. Begin at the Great Forest Trees Walk trailhead sign, 3.9 kilometres north of the Shannon campsite. Shannon National Park is unique in the South-West forests because, together with the adjoining D'Entrecasteaux National Park, it protects the entire catchment area of the Shannon River. This means that the river and stream system and the underground water flowing through the forest all drain into national parks and are protected by the forested catchment. The 53 500 hectare park includes some of the most magnificent karri country in WA. The area was logged between the mid-1940s and 1983 and gazetted as a national park in December 1988.
2. You need to negotiate stepping stones to cross the Shannon River. Pure stands of karri, with its smooth white bark and towering trunk, line the walk at this point. Karri is a water-loving species and dominates the forest in the best-watered areas. In shallower and less fertile areas on upper slopes, it often grows in association with marri and jarrah. The Shannon River was named not long after the Swan River Colony was established in 1829. A few years earlier, Britain and America had come to blows over Britain's policy of searching neutral ships bound for Europe, an attempt to break Napoleon's supply lines. In 1813, Sir Philip Broke led the Royal Navy's *Shannon* into battle against the American frigate, *Chesapeake*, off the coast of New England. Britain's victory was commemorated in the naming of the Shannon River, and also at nearby Broke Inlet and Chesapeake Road.
3. The rest of the walk continues through karri forest. The best time to see wildflowers is from October to December. White clematis, a common creeper of the South-West forests, often grows with the purple pea flowers of native

wisteria, the yellow blooms of the wattle prickly moses and the vibrant reddish-orange pea flowers of coral vine, creating a magnificent display of blue, yellow, red and white.

4. About 2.8 kilometres along the trail you will cross a tributary to the Shannon River, which, like the Shannon, only flows in winter time.

Where is it? *The beginning of the trail is about 60 km south of Manjimup, 70 km north of Walpole and 36 km from Northcliffe. It lies on the Upper Shannon Road, north-east of the Shannon campsite.*
Travelling time: *50 minutes from Manjimup and Walpole or 35 minutes from Pemberton.*
Facilities: *Car park.*
Best season: *All year.*

Cliff Winfield

THE GREAT FOREST TREES DRIVE

The Great Forest Trees Drive, in Shannon National Park, was established in 1996. This 48 kilometre drive takes in some of the most spectacular old growth karri forest in the South-West, and is punctuated with six picnic and information stops, and two walks.

The Great Forest Trees Drive starts north of the South Western Highway, just beyond the shingled roof information shelter and the turn-off to the covered barbecue areas and walktrails. Before proceeding, visitors often stop and read the information at the shelter, walk to the dam or have a barbecue lunch. The roads for the drive are not sealed but are suitable for conventional vehicles and small coaches. Great Forest Trees Drive signs show the way from the information shelter onto Upper Shannon Road and indicate where visitors should tune in their car radios to hear broadcasts about the area on a special park radio circuit.

After following the one way northern loop for 23 kilometres, the Drive crosses the highway into the lower Shannon area, where the roads are once again two way. After visiting Snake Gully lookout and Big Tree Grove, where you can see karri giants, the drive returns along the river to the old Shannon townsite. The loop ends where it begins, on South Western Highway.

5
STEEP TRAIL
CLAMBER UP
ROCK FACE
SOUTHERN OCEAN
4
3
SWAMPS
2
CAR
PARK
PICNIC
AREA
1
ENTRY

Mount Chudalup

D'Entrecasteaux National Park

27

Length: *1 km return.*
Grade: *3.*
Walk time: *30 minutes.*

This is a very scenic, moderate to steep, but not overly strenuous, walk. From the top you can enjoy sweeping views of the coast and surrounds including the Meerup and Doggerup Dunes, the Southern Ocean, and D'Entrecasteaux and Shannon national parks.

1. Begin at the Mount Chudalup car park. Tall karri and marri trees surround the first section of the trail, with an attractive understorey of chorilaena (*Chorilaena quercifolia*), tassel bush (*Leucopogon verticillatis*), bracken fern (*Pteridium esculentum*) and zamia palm (*Macrozamia reidleii*).
2. Turn right when you reach the blackboy and marri fringed rock. Cross two small bridges then make your way over bare rock.
3. You must cross a further two small bridges between bare granite areas. Blackboys and sheoak trees inhabit small pockets of soil.
4. The final section of path is quite steep and you must clamber up the rock face to reach the top. It is not too strenuous, however, because the trail is relatively short and Mount Chudalup lies only 163 metres above sea level.
5. On the top take some time to enjoy great views. You can see the patterns of the land which give D'Entrecasteaux its unique character. It is a transition between the coastal belt and the tall forests. Continual lashing by Southern Ocean winds has created an extensive sand dune system. These coastal dunes have blocked the flow of streams and creeks trying to empty into the ocean. Over time, this has created a chain of lakes and wetlands extending from Broke Inlet in the south to Lake Jasper (the largest freshwater lake in the South-West) north of here. Examine the unusual plant communities perched on Mount Chudalup. Melaleucas and other stunted plants have created what looks like miniature "rock gardens".
6. Retrace your steps to the car park.

Where is it? *15 km south of Northcliffe on the Windy Harbour Road.*
Travelling time: *10 minutes from Northcliffe.*
Best season: *Spring for wildflowers.*

Tammie Reid

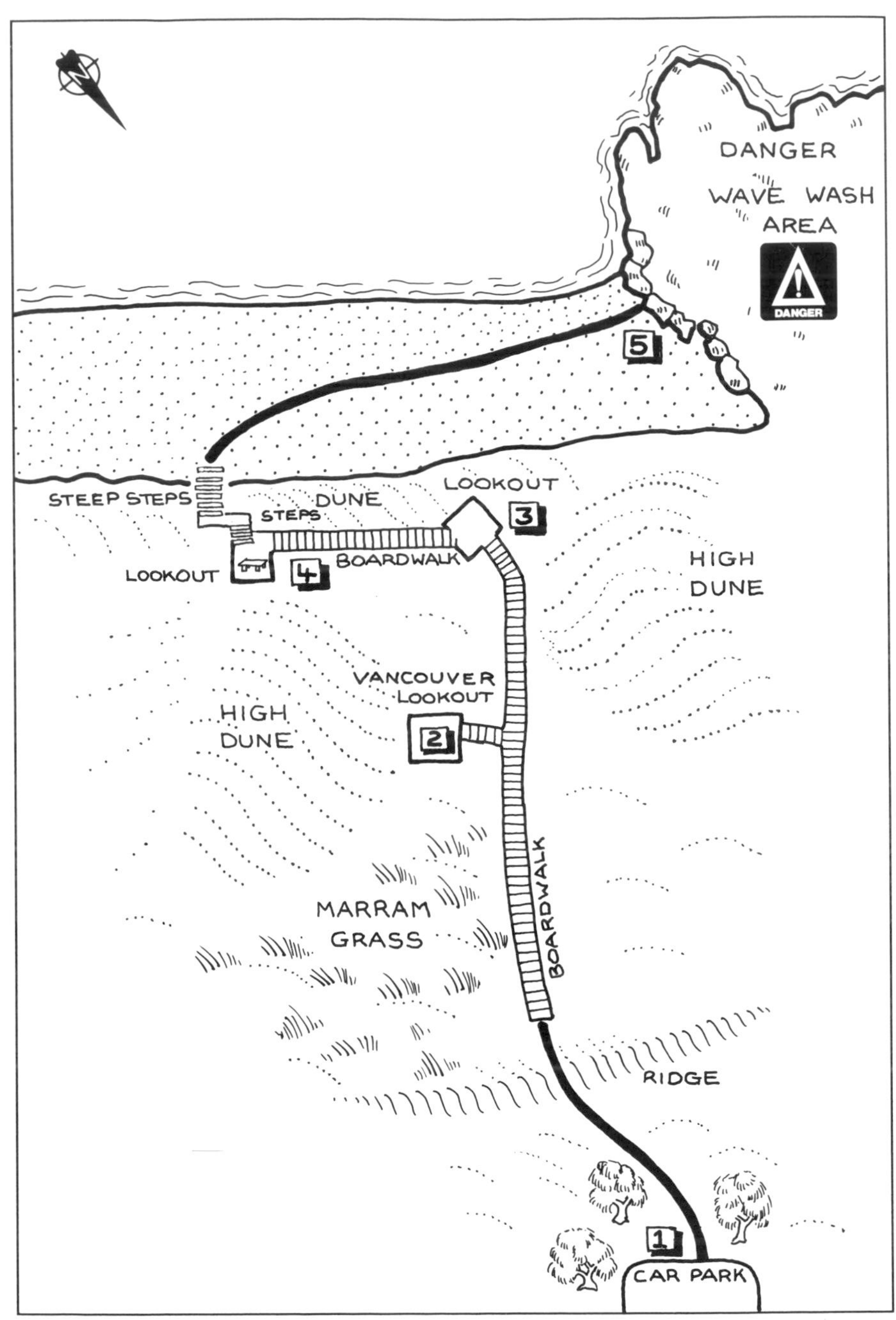
DANGER
WAVE WASH
AREA
DANGER
5
LOOKOUT
3
STEEP STEPS
DUNE
STEPS
BOARDWALK
HIGH
DUNE
LOOKOUT
4
VANCOUVER
LOOKOUT
HIGH
DUNE
2
MARRAM
GRASS
BOARDWALK
RIDGE
1
CAR PARK

Mandalay Beach

D'Entrecasteaux National Park

Length: *1 km return.*
Grade: *2.*
Walk time: *30 minutes to an hour.*

Mandalay Beach is one of only three coastal sites in D'Entrecasteaux National Park accessible by conventional vehicle. This lovely place can be reached via a gravel track through coastal and peppermint woodlands and relict dune sequences. The walk from the car park to the beach is part of the long distance Bibbulmun Track, which continues east along the beach and thence to Walpole and Albany.

1. Begin at the car park and follow the narrow dirt track that winds through the swale of the dunes. Plants such as peppermint, native rosemary, Australian bluebell, native wisteria and coastal pigface have found a foothold in the dunes.
2. After traversing a ridge, head down along a boardwalk through marram grass (a plant introduced to stabilise the dunes) to the first lookout nestled between high dunes. The lookout gives great views over Chatham Island.
3. Another lookout, 200 metres from the start, gives views over the secluded sandy beach. The beach takes its name from the 914 ton Norwegian barque *Mandalay*, wrecked here in 1911. An information post, adorned with a cast of the ship's figurehead, has extracts from the diary of Captain Emile Tonessen. The wreck appears from shifting sands every few years.
4. A lengthy boardwalk incorporating steep stairs takes you to the beach, flanked at each end by rocky points. Walk to the rocks on your right. Keep away from the steep sand dunes that fringe the beach as sand slides pose a very real danger.
5. If you decide to climb the rocks, take great care and keep well above the wave wash area, even on calm days. From the rocks you can view a small sandy beach strewn with weathered boulders. Behind the beach, the basement geology of granitic rocks and their overlying strata of limestone is well exposed. Retrace your steps.

Where is it? *The turn-off to Mandalay Beach Road is 13 km west of Walpole, and the beach is another 10 km or so.*
Travelling time: *30 minutes from Walpole.*
Facilities: *Lookouts, information.*
Best season: *Spring and summer.*

Carolyn Thomson and Peter Dans

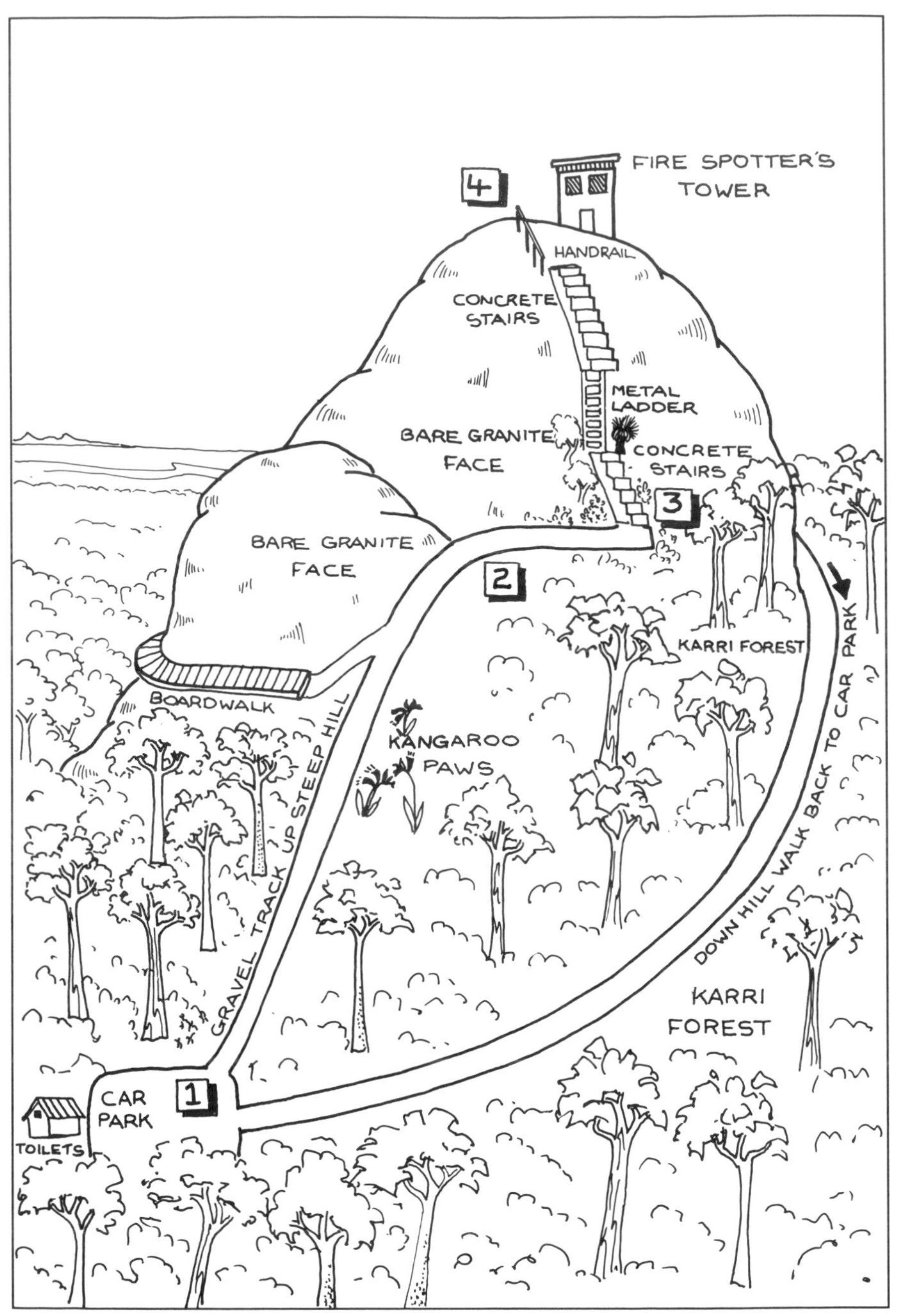
FIRE SPOTTER'S TOWER
4
HANDRAIL
CONCRETE STAIRS
METAL LADDER
BARE GRANITE FACE
CONCRETE STAIRS
3
BARE GRANITE FACE
2
KARRI FOREST
BOARDWALK
GRAVEL TRACK UP STEEP HILL
KANGAROO PAWS
DOWN HILL WALK BACK TO CAR PARK
KARRI FOREST
CAR PARK
1
TOILETS

Mount Frankland

29

Mount Frankland National Park

***Length:** 2 km return.*
***Grade:** 3.*
***Walk time:** $1^1/_2$ hours.*

Mount Frankland boasts some of the most breathtaking scenery of all the walks in this book. It should not be missed.

1. Begin at the car park in Mount Frankland National Park. Tall karri and marri trees surround the trail, with a lush understorey that includes tassel bush, bracken fern, green kangaroo paws, white clematis (*Clematis pubescens*) and snottygobble trees (*Persoonia longifolia*).
2. You will soon arrive at a sheer, mossy face of granite. Ignore the path to the left and turn right to continue upward, around the base of the granite outcrop.
3. Narrow concrete steps wind steeply upward, through small pockets of soil and vegetation. Bullich (*Eucalyptus megacarpa*) grows alongside the steps. Like karri, this smooth-barked tree sheds its old grey bark to reveal mottled tonings of yellow, pink, orange, pale grey and white, but it does not grow as tall as karri and has much larger fruits.
4. You have to negotiate steep metal stairs and steep concrete steps to reach the summit of Mount Frankland, 411 metres above sea level. On top is an operational fire spotting tower. On a clear day you can see the Stirling and Porongurup Ranges and Chatham Island, near Walpole. The granite monadnock to the north is Mount Roe and the flat hill to its left is Mount Mitchell.
5. After enjoying the incredible views, return down the steps and skirt around the base of the bare granite face until you reach the path you passed earlier. Take this path, which initially traverses a boardwalk over the bare granite and then makes its way around the base of Mount Frankland through beautiful karri forest sprinkled with wildflowers. The views are delightful, and the path is an easy grade (mostly downhill). It will return you direct to the car park.

***Where is it?** 27 km north of Walpole via North Walpole Road and Mt Frankland Road. The gravel road to the park is quite corrugated and slippery in places, so please take care.*
***Travelling time:** 30-40 minutes.*

Carolyn Thomson and Peter Dans

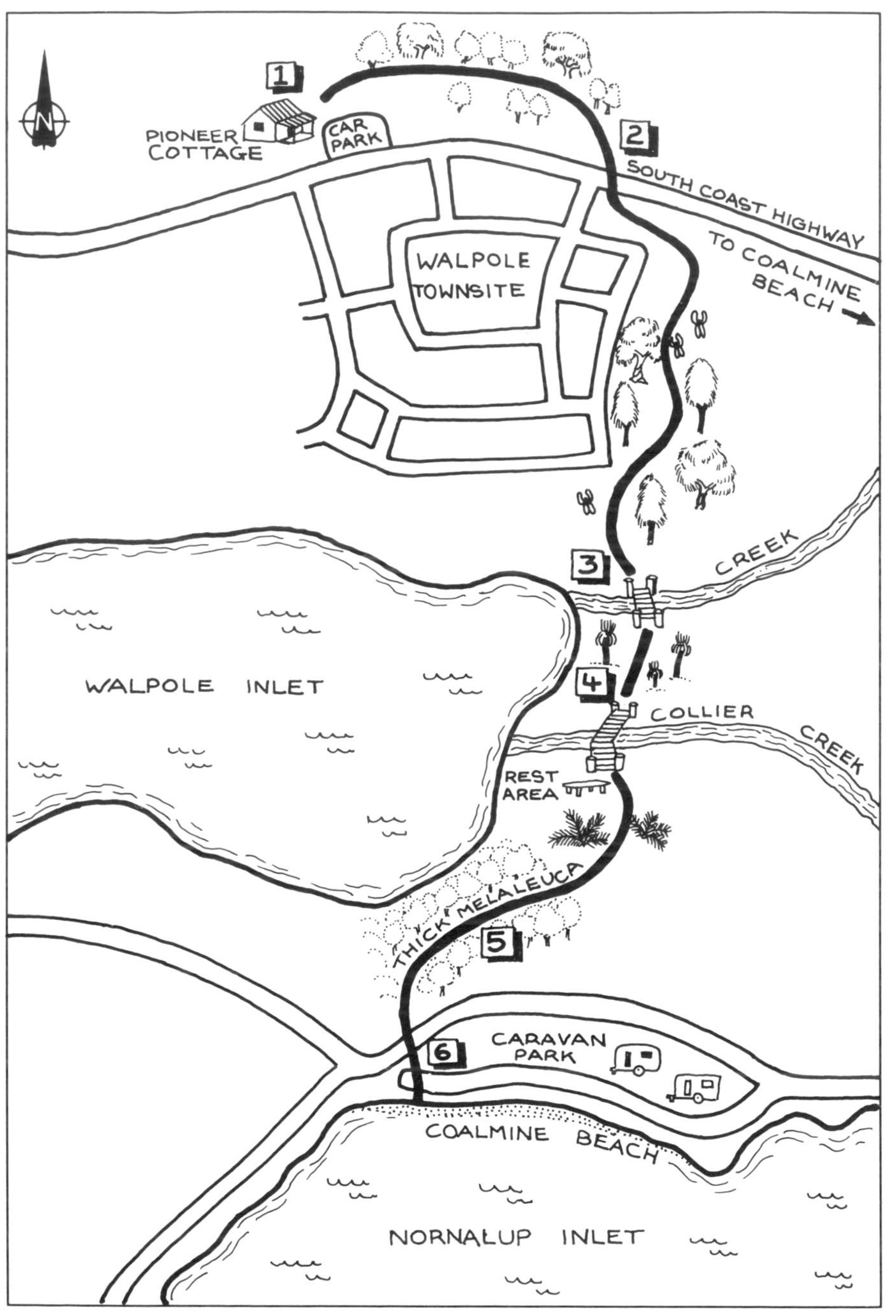
1
PIONEER COTTAGE
CAR PARK
2
SOUTH COAST HIGHWAY
TO COALMINE BEACH
WALPOLE TOWNSITE
3
CREEK
WALPOLE INLET
4
COLLIER CREEK
REST AREA
THICK MELALEUCA
5
6
CARAVAN PARK
COALMINE BEACH
NORNALUP INLET

Coalmine Beach

30

Bibbulmun Track, Walpole-Nornalup National Park

Length: *6 km return.*
Grade: *2.*
Walk time: *2 hours.*

This trail runs from the town of Walpole, through woodland and wetlands to Coalmine Beach. Interpretive signs convey how a teenager from an early settlement family may have experienced the environment through which the trail passes. From August 1998, the trail is to form part of the realigned Bibbulmun Track, which travels east to Albany.

1. Begin at the Pioneer Cottage on the northern side of the South Western Highway in Walpole. In October 1930, a small community of tents and tin and bushpole shanties was established in this area, marking the beginning of the Nornalup Land Settlement, later to become known as Walpole. Those attracted to the scheme lived in a makeshift main camp, where Pioneer Park now stands, until blocks of 120 acres (47.6 hectares) of forested land were allocated to each family by ballot. The first section of the walk is through scrub of melaleucas and peppermint. Bracken fern (*Pteridium esculentum*) grows here profusely. This is a native species and not introduced as is commonly thought.
2. Cross the road, taking care to avoid traffic. The vegetation near the road is composed mainly of taller peppermint trees and sheoak. You should be able to locate two plaques that describe the uses put to blackboys and other plants by early settlers. The track branches twice but take the left hand trail each time. As you begin to descend slightly, see if you can locate the climbing triggerplant, with its delicate pink flowers which appear from June to February. Triggerplant flowers have sensitive columns that flick over at the slightest touch and dab pollen on visiting insects.
3. Traverse a bridge that crosses a small creek. Continue along the track until you reach an impressive 7-8 metre high kingia (*Kingia australis*). The kingia resembles the blackboy but the two species belong to different families.
4. Negotiate the creek by means of a boardwalk, followed by a shady rest area under some eucalypts. You should be able to spot zamia palms, en route to the next point of interest.
5. Near the end of the walk you will pass through a swampy area inhabited by dense thickets of melaleucas and bracken ferns. There is a plaque about the quokka, which once lived in the area.

6. Cross another road, adjacent to the Coalmine Beach Caravan Park, to complete the walk at Coalmine Beach on the Nornalup Inlet. An Aboriginal tribe known as the Minang originally occupied the area from Albany north to the Stirling Range and west to the Shannon River and Broke Inlet. They called the larger inlet Nornalup, meaning "place of the tiger snake".

Where is it? *The national park surrounds the town of Walpole.*
Travelling time: *Right in the town of Walpole.*
Facilities: *There are picnic tables, barbecues and a playground at the Pioneer Park at the start of the walk. There is also a day use site with a barbecue and tables at Coalmine Beach.*
Best season: *All year.*

RED-FLOWERING GUM

When flowering, this irregular, straggly and somewhat nondescript tree is transformed into a blaze of colour. The prolific blooms vary from brilliant scarlet and crimson through oranges and pinks, to a delicate shade of the palest pink. Understandably, red-flowering gum (*Corymbia ficifolia*) is highly prized as an ornamental eucalypt and is cultivated all over the world. In the wild, however, the gum is found only from near Mt Frankland to Walpole and east to Denmark. There is an isolated population east of Albany.

Red-flowering gum is a small tree up to 10 metres high. It has rough, greyish-brown bark similar to that of marri. The leaves are shiny dark green above and paler below, and have veins packed together like those of marri. Stunning flowers appear from summer to early autumn. The large, woody fruits are barrel-shaped to very slightly urn-shaped and contract at the opening.

Red-flowering gum is one of the most commonly grown ornamental eucalypts outside WA. When grown in WA, however, this species is very prone to stem canker, a fungal disease, which killed most of the early plantings. Marri (*Corymbia calophylla*) is more resistant, so most "red-flowering gums" in Perth are hybrids with marri.

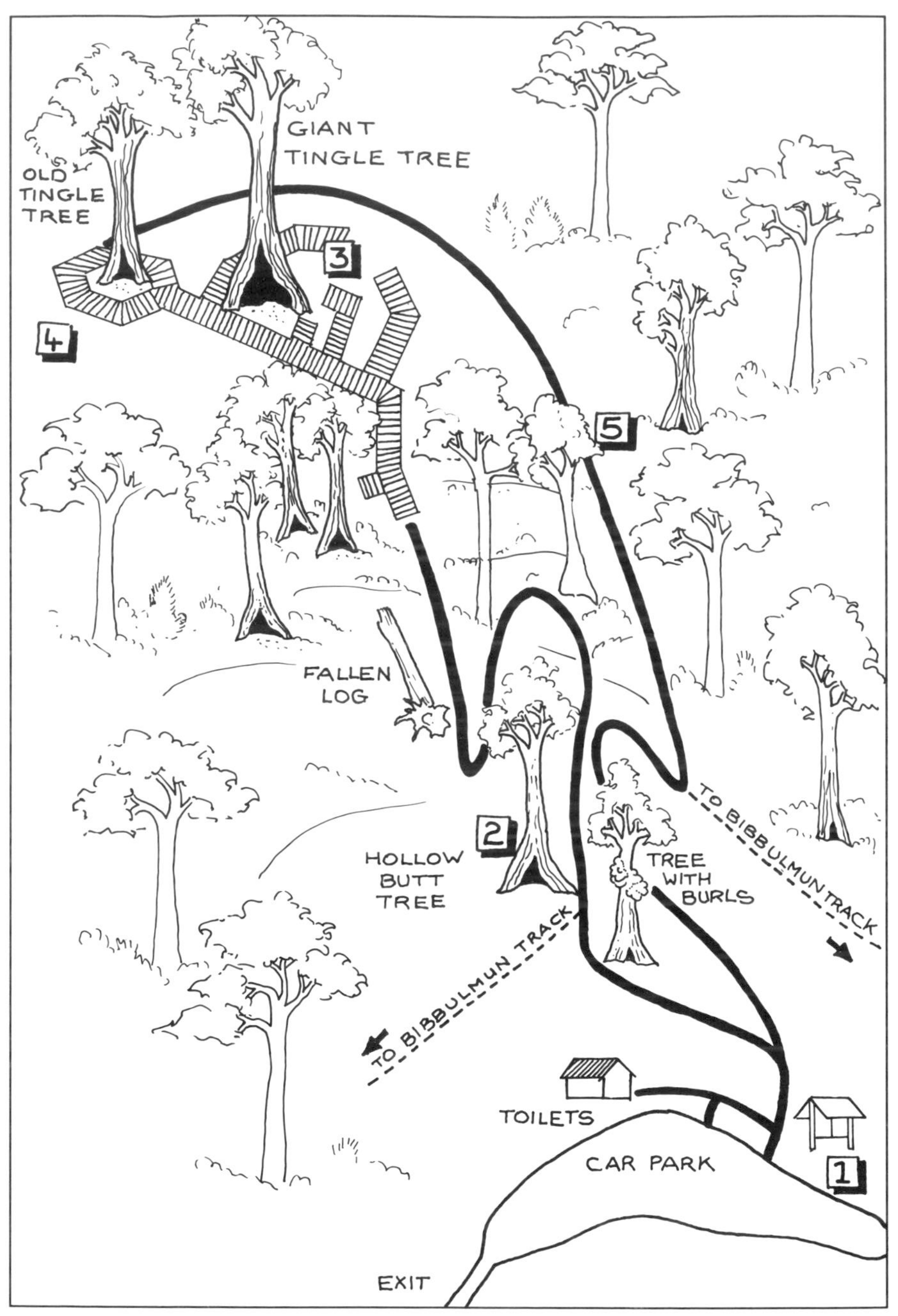

GIANT
TINGLE TREE
OLD
TINGLE
TREE
3
4
5
FALLEN
LOG
2
HOLLOW
BUTT
TREE
TREE
WITH
BURLS
TO BIBBULMUN TRACK
TO BIBBULMUN TRACK
TOILETS
CAR PARK
1
EXIT

Hilltop Giant Tingle Tree Trail 31

Walpole-Nornalup National Park

Length: *800 m.*
Grade: *1.*
Walk time: *40-50 minutes.*

The Hilltop area is in spectacular forest just minutes from Walpole. The Giant Tingle Tree is a large, old tree that has, over many years, been hollowed out by fire. It is possible to negotiate the path with a wheelchair but it is recommended that a fairly strong, fit person be present to assist because of the moderately steep slope.

1. Follow the path from the car park to the information shelter. Then take the path to the left where the arrow indicates the way to the Giant Tingle Tree. The trail winds downhill through karri and tingle forest, with an understorey including tassel bush, karri wattle and bracken fern. Karri sheoak groves can be seen in several places along the whole trail.
2. Signs along the path give information on tree species, burls, birds and on nutrient and biological cycles in the tingle forest. As the path curves down the slope, you may pause at one of several rest areas provided with bench seats.
3. At the bottom of the hill you reach a boardwalk that surrounds the Giant Tingle Tree. From the boardwalk you can also see deep into the forest.
4. Continue along the boardwalk to a second majestic tingle tree. Once you walk up the steps and around the tree you will see that the trail leads off the boardwalk behind it. If you brought a pusher or wheelchair you can return the way you came and avoid the steps.
5. Signs along the path help you to identify and learn about the forest birds. The path divides at one point and you need to follow the right hand part back to the car park, as indicated by a small sign. As you drive out of the car park, you can either drive a further six kilometres to Circular Pool on the Frankland River or return to the highway via the road to your right.

Where is it? *The turn-off to Hilltop Road is 2 km east of Walpole on the north side of South Coast Highway, directly opposite the road to Coalmine Beach. The gravel road is one way and the car park is 5 km from the highway.*
Facilities: *Picnic tables and toilets, with access for the disabled.*
Best season: *All year.*

Anna Gemer

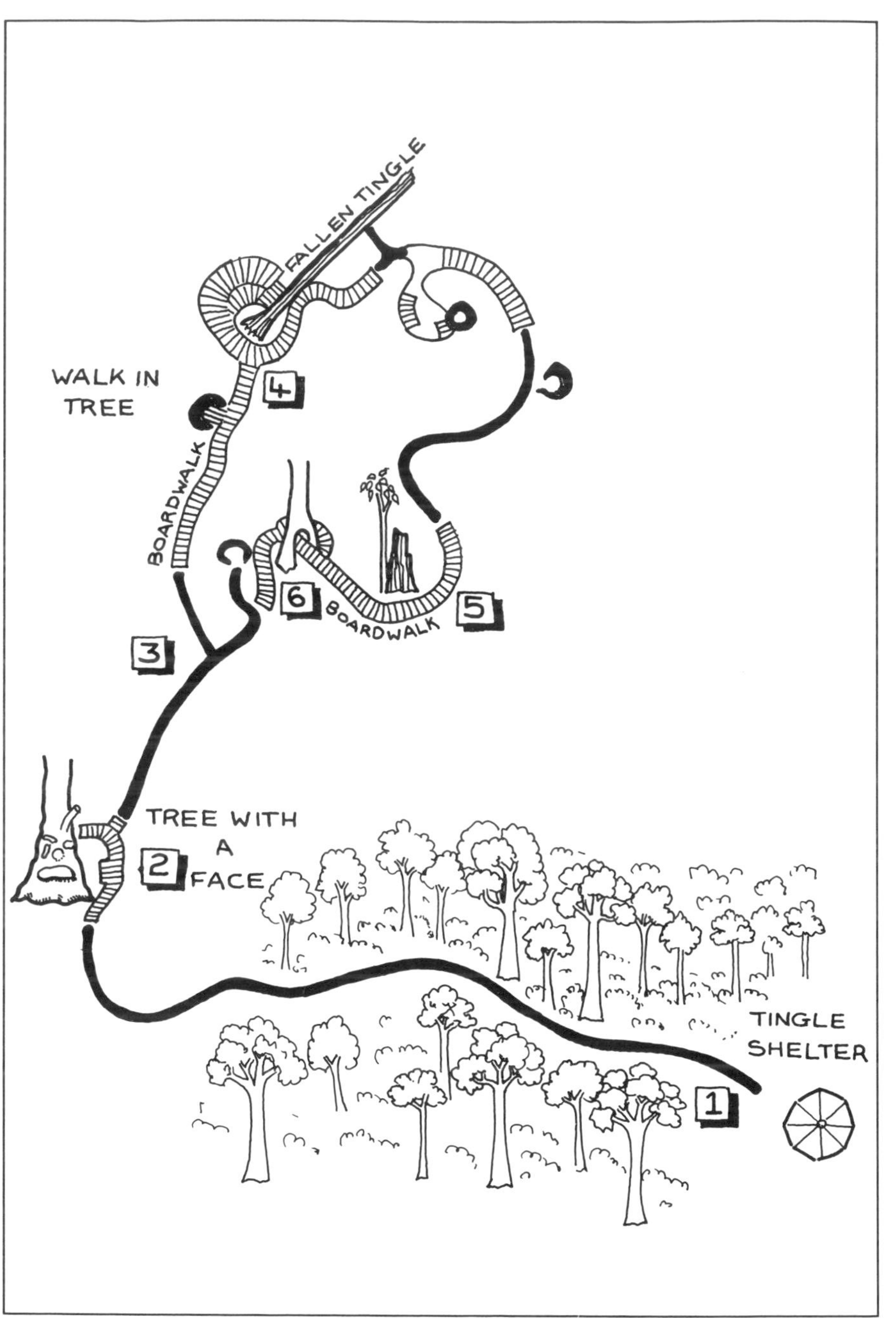
FALLEN TINGLE
WALK IN
TREE
4
BOARDWALK
6
BOARDWALK
5
3
TREE WITH
A
FACE
2
TINGLE
SHELTER
1

Valley of the Giants Ancient Empire Trail

32

Walpole-Nornalup National Park

Length: *800 m.*
Grade: *1.*
Walk time: *20-30 minutes.*

Walpole-Nornalup National Park is known for three rare and wonderful eucalypts - the red, yellow and Rate's tingles. The park's Valley of the Giants - one of WA's favourite tourist stops for decades - features a boardwalk and rammed earth trail over the forest floor. The first 100 metres are wheelchair accessible. After finishing, you can then experience a stunning Tree Top Walk through the tingle forest canopy.

1. Begin at the Tingle Shelter. Tall karri and marri trees surround the trail, with a lush understorey that includes tassel bush (*Leucopogon verticillatis*), bracken fern (*Pteridium esculentum*) and karri wattle (*Acacia pentadenia*). Karri sheoak (*Allocasuarina decussata*) can be recognised by its moss-covered, thick, corky bark.
2. Red tingles are the most massive of all eucalypts. Though not as tall as karri trees, they are known for their huge buttressed trunks, which have circumferences of up to 20 metres. Red tingle trees can grow up to 60 metres tall. These rare and lovely trees grow only in the lower catchment areas of the Deep, Frankland and Bow Rivers, where they intermingle with karri, yellow tingle and Rate's tingle. The first point of interest is a red tingle tree that appears to have a face on its gnarled trunk. The boardwalk curls part way around it so that you can have a closer look without contributing to compaction of its sensitive root system. Watch for birds, such as splendid wrens, nearby.
3. Take the right hand option where the track forks. A long section of boardwalk incorporates a tingle tree that you can walk into. Red tingle trees have often suffered damage from past wildfires, when deep leaf litter and fallen logs around their base have burnt through the bark and left scars of dead wood. The trees continue to grow around the scar, but the next fire will burn away the dead wood. After centuries of fires, a huge hollow eventually develops which often occupies most of the enlarged base of the trunk.
4. A viewing platform takes you around and above a large fallen tingle tree, so that you can see its twisted roots and massive size more easily.
5. Another section of boardwalk takes you beneath an archway formed by two tingle trees and past an old tree with a hollowed out and burnt base that has, amazingly, sent up a new shoot.

6. Examine another walk-through tree before rejoining the first section of trail and returning to the Tingle Shelter past the tree with a face.

Where is it? *The turn-off to the Valley of the Giants Road is 14 km east of Walpole.*
Travelling time: *20 minutes from Walpole.*
Facilities: *Toilets, information panels, souvenir shop, Tree Top Walk.*
Best season: *All year.*

Cliff Winfield and Carolyn Thomson

TINGLE TREES

Red tingle trees (*Eucalyptus jacksonii*) are the most massive of all eucalypts. They reach up to 70 metres tall and have huge buttressed trunks up to 20 metres in circumference. Red tingle trunks are often split and internally burnt by past wildfires, leaving a huge hollow which often occupies most of the enlarged base of the trunk. One much photographed tree had a hollow base large enough to drive a car into, but unfortunately it fell down a few years ago.

These trees can be seen at their best in the Valley of the Giants, in Walpole-Nornalup National Park, where you can even walk through the tree tops of the massive trees. Many are believed to be more than 400 years old. Their bark is rough, stringy and grey to brown in colour. White blossoms appear in summer.

There are three types of tingle trees, all confined to the wetter South-West. The others are yellow tingle (*Eucalyptus guilfoylei*) and Rate's tingle (*Eucalyptus brevistylis*). Tingle trees are relicts from a period 65 million years ago, when Australia was part of the supercontinent Gondwana and the climate was warm and continuously wet. Tingles are now found only in the Walpole-Nornalup area, which has the wettest and least seasonal climate in the South-West.

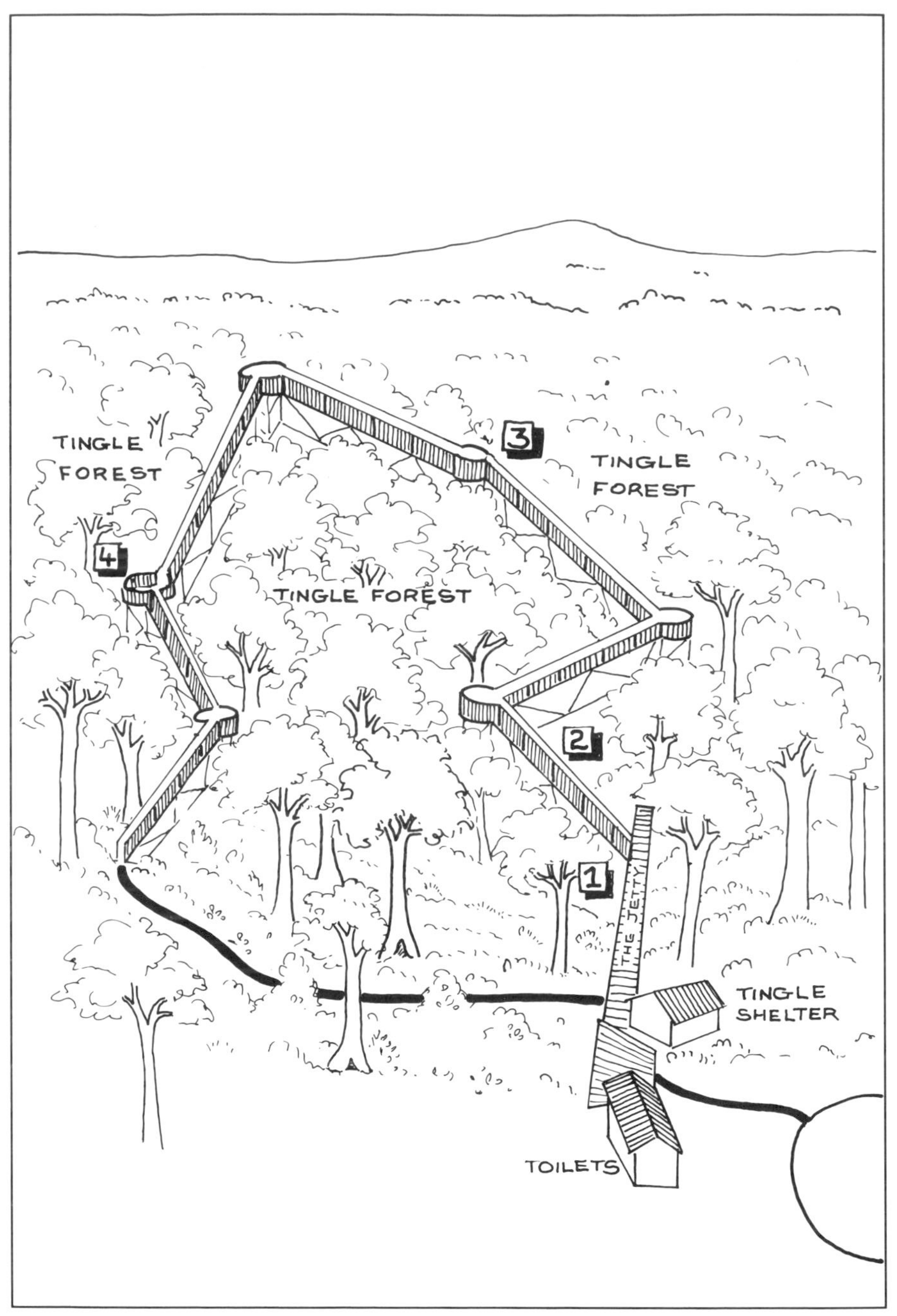
TINGLE
FOREST
3
TINGLE
FOREST
4
TINGLE FOREST
2
1
THE JETTY
TINGLE
SHELTER
TOILETS

Tree Top Walk

33

Walpole-Nornalup National Park ($)

Brilliant! 8/1/98
$12 per family. Fascinating structure.

Length: *600 m.*
Grade: *1.*
Walk time: *20 minutes.*

The Tree Top Walk provides an exciting and different perspective on the shapes, sounds and movement of the rare tingle forest. It is the world's only tree top walk in tall eucalypt forest and with a rigid structure. It comprises a series of lightweight bridge spans, each 60 metres long and four metres deep, supported between pylons. The walkway rises with no steps, on a gentle grade suitable for children, wheelchairs and the elderly, up to 40 metres above the forest floor, where it crosses a valley. There is a charge for going on the Tree Top Walk.

1. Ascending into the crowns of the giants is easy. After the first solid section known as the "jetty" you are already above the understorey. The walkway was specially designed to minimise disturbance to the natural environment and, remarkably, the pylons only occupy around three square metres of the forest floor. The sculptural design of the trusses mimics the natural form of sword grass, a predominant local plant species, while the pylons resemble the tassel flower.
2. From the jetty you embark onto the one-way section of walkway. At ground level, purple-crowned lorikeets provide mere background chatter and squeaks. On the Tree Top Walk you share their lofty space, as they whizz past you in search of nectar. At eye level, pardalotes and treecreepers fossick and turn leaves and bark in search of insects. The valley's 'giants' are the red tingles (*Eucalyptus jacksonii*). The word 'tingle' comes from an Aboriginal term and 'red' is for the almost purple colour of its timber.
3. Soon the bridge spans reach a height of 40 metres above the creek bed. Up close, branches in the canopy of the tingle trees turn out to be a metre thick, and there is a constant rush of breeze through the leaves. From here you gain an impressive view over farmland and forest, towards the dome of Mount Frankland.
4. Descend to the ground and return to the start.

Where is it? *The Valley of the Giants Road turn-off is 14 km east of Walpole.*
Travelling time: *20 minutes from Walpole.*
Facilities: *Toilets, information, souvenir shop.*
Best season: *All year.*

Cliff Winfield

CAR
PARK
DENMARK
9km
1
2
3
SCOTSDALE CREEK
SCOTSDALE ROAD

Harewood Forest

Denmark

34

Length: *1.2 km return.*
Grade: *1.*
Walk time: *20-30 minutes.*

The car park on the northern side of Scotsdale Road is marked by Heritage Trail sign no.7. It is an easy 1.2 km walk winding through karri forest on the banks of the Scotsdale Brook to a picnic setting. Trailside plaques along the way tell the story of this unique island of karri amongst the farmland and help you to identify some of the common plants of the karri forest.

1. From the car park, the trail leads down to a footbridge across the Scotsdale Creek.
2. Above the creek to the right is a picnic table, but the trail turns left before this and runs alongside the creek for about 600 metres, ending at a second picnic table down near the creek. The trail meanders through regrowth karri forest. This area was milled in the late 1800s and allowed to regenerate, whereas the surrounding areas were taken up as farmland.
3. Return by the same route. This is a rewarding area for birdwatchers. Birds you are likely to see include the cobalt blue splendid wren, the white-breasted robin, golden whistler, crested shrike-tit and red-winged fairy-wren. Red-tailed and Baudin's (white-tailed) black-cockatoos can often be seen overhead.

Where is it? *9.3 km from Denmark along Scotsdale Road.*
Travelling time: *15 minutes from Denmark.*
Facilities: *Picnic tables are located at both ends of the walk.*
Best season: *Spring.*

Graham Hick

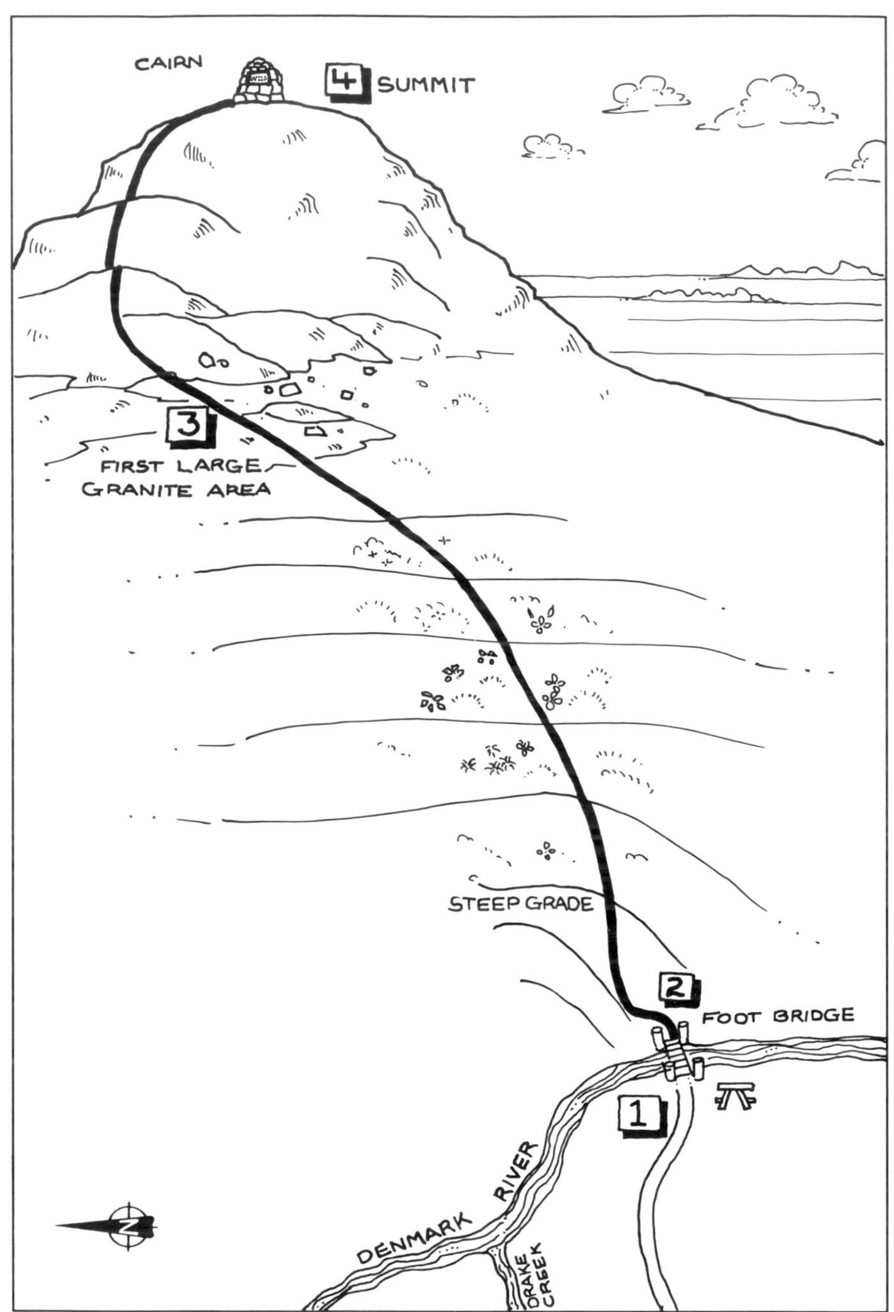
CAIRN
4 SUMMIT
3
FIRST LARGE
GRANITE AREA
STEEP GRADE
2
FOOT BRIDGE
1
DENMARK RIVER
DRAKE CREEK
N

Mt Lindesay

35

Denmark

Length: *8 km.*
Grade: *3.*
Walk time: *3 hours.*

The walk trail up Mount Lindesay climbs for about four kilometres from the Denmark River to the 400-metre-high granite dome visible to the north of the town. Follow the signposts on Scotsdale Road and along Mount Lindesay Road, past the Emu Farm to the junction of Break and Nutcracker Roads. Turn right and continue to the parking area at the river, 22 kilometres from town.

The indicated time of three hours does not allow for adequate appreciation of the magnificent flora. This is at its best in late spring, but there are some plants in bloom during all seasons, and they change continuously as the track ascends. Many species are endemic to the area, which has been proposed as a national park.

1. A track above the parking area leads to picnic tables and to a footbridge over the river.
2. Across the river make a sharp left hand turn to the walk track. Though the track is quite steep for the first 500 metres it is then an easy grade for about 2.5 kilometres to the first large granite area.
3. After the granite, the track is steeper and is marked on the rock by painted arrows.
4. At the summit a panoramic view sweeps from Mount Frankland to the west and east to the Porongurup Range, Stirling Range and Mount Manypeaks. A plaque on the cairn provides historical information.
5. Return by the same route.

Where is it? *22 km from Denmark via Scotsdale and Mount Lindesay Roads.*
Travelling time: *20 minutes from Denmark.*
Facilities: *Car park, picnic tables.*
Best season: *All year.*

Lola Broadhurst, Brenda Hammersley, Jennifer Young and Jessie MacIver

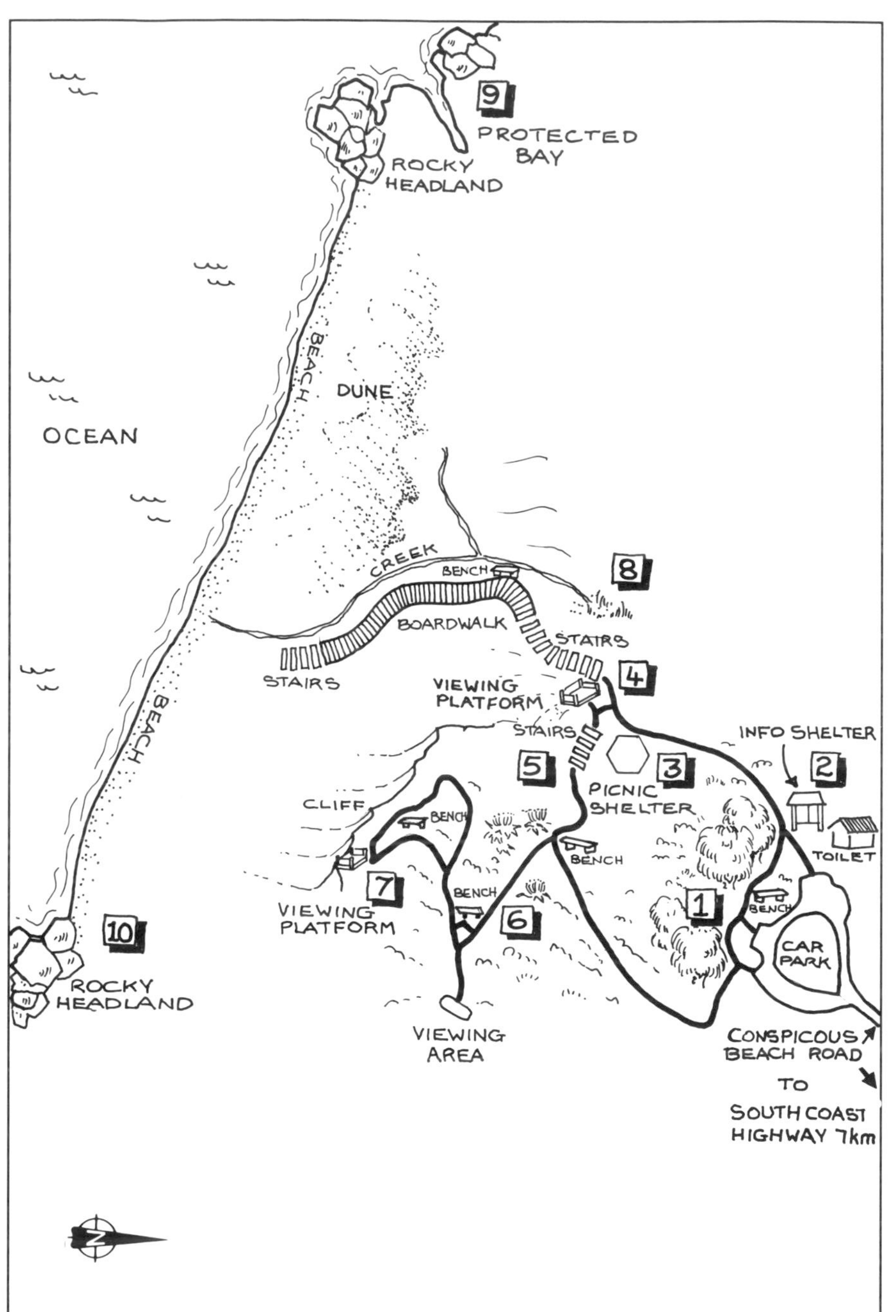
9
PROTECTED BAY
ROCKY HEADLAND
BEACH
DUNE
OCEAN
CREEK
BENCH
8
BOARDWALK
STAIRS
STAIRS
4
VIEWING PLATFORM
STAIRS
INFO SHELTER
2
5
3
PICNIC SHELTER
CLIFF
BENCH
TOILET
BENCH
7
BENCH
1
BENCH
VIEWING PLATFORM
6
CAR PARK
10
ROCKY HEADLAND
BEACH
VIEWING AREA
CONSPICOUS BEACH ROAD
TO
SOUTH COAST HIGHWAY 7km
N

Conspicuous Beach Walks **36**

Walpole-Nornalup National Park

Lengths: *200 m return - Picnic shelter and first lookout platform (accessible to all); 650 m return - Whalewatch lookout; or 800 m return - Beach Walk.*
Grade: *1 to 2.*

These walks feature outstanding views from a limestone knoll, a stunning beach and rocky headlands. By August 1998, medium and longer walks via the new Bibbulmun Track will be available. You will be able to continue east along the coast to the highest point on Conspicuous Cliff and onwards to Peaceful Bay or walk north to experience country featuring red-flowering gum, and the magnificent tingle forest at the Valley of the Giants.

1. Begin at the car park and head for the information shelter. The hardened footpath winds through shady Warren River cedar (*Agonis juniperina*) and coastal heath, with several species of cream-coloured hakeas, yellow wattles and hibbertia species, the greyish-blue foliage of native rosemary (*Olearia axillaris*), and the striking purple flowers of native wisteria (*Hardenbergia comptoniana*). There is a bench on which to sit and observe the wrens, robins and honeyeaters that frequent this spot.
2. Another bench near the information shelter and toilet offers views to the prominent limestone feature known as Conspicuous Cliffs, a kilometre (as the crow flies) to the east.
3. Continue past the information shelter for 80 metres to a covered hexagonal picnic shelter, a welcome shelter from summer heat. It is also ideal for waiting for winter squalls, which are often short-lived, to clear.
4. A short walk leads to the first lookout, which has ocean views, and overlooks a permanent spring-fed stream which flows to the beach. Up to this point, the track is accessible to visitors of all abilities, including those in wheelchairs. Sometimes elderly visitors spend their time here while younger visitors continue the walk.
5. The stairs leading upwards traverse a steep section of bush and, from the top of another hardened track, winds around the base of the knoll to a bench at a junction in the track. Ignore the track to the left (you may wish to use it later to return to the car park via another route) and continue up the slope. Several more rest stops with benches are located on the journey. Along the walk you may notice the prickly-leaved parrotbush (*Dryandra sessilis*), the woolly-needled grey stinkwood (*Jacksonia furcellata*), berry saltbush (*Rhagodia baccata*), with its bright red berries, and various orchid species.

6. At a sharp switch-back ramp, another junction offers a spur track to the left, which terminates at a bench from which to watch the sea in the distance and observe a prominent sand blowout stretching two kilometres inland between two razorback ridges.
7. Take the track to the right, which arrives via a circuit loop to the main whalewatch platform. From here, all parts of the beach are visible, bordered on both sides by rocky headlands. Whales are frequently spotted in winter and spring. As they are sometimes some distance out, scan the area with binoculars to look for the white spray sent up from their 'blowholes'. Dolphins are often seen near the surface, surfing the waves together in pods of a dozen or more.
8. Return to the stairs and this time continue down to the junction of two springs, which form a stream flowing into the sea. Walk alongside this shallow stream, or take the boardwalk along its edge onto the beach. Swimming is not recommended here, as there is always a strong undertow or 'rip', which can carry swimmers out to sea.
9. Rocky headlands, 200 metres to the west, can be negotiated with care, provided you stay well away from the wave zone. You will come to a narrow bay which is open to the sea. It is relatively safe for a swim, but beware, even this relatively protected bay experiences strong surges which could carry a swimmer out to sea.
10. To the east, the beach ends at a rocky headland. A marker will show the access point from here to the Bibbulmun Track, which will soon continue inland from the sand blowout, via Conspicuous Cliff to Peaceful Bay and on to Albany.
11. Return to the car park via the stairs and footpath.

Where is it? *The turn-off is found along the South-Western Highway, 500 m east of the turn-off to the Valley of the Giants. Conspicuous Beach Road then heads some 10 km south to the car park.*
Travelling time: *30 minutes from Walpole or 20 minutes from Nornalup or Peaceful Bay.*
Facilities: *Car park, toilets and picnic shelter.*
Best season: *Winter and spring for whales and wildflowers, summer for beach activities and surfing, autumn for salmon fishing.*

Charlie Salamon

Mountains and Sea Cliffs Walks 37 - 44

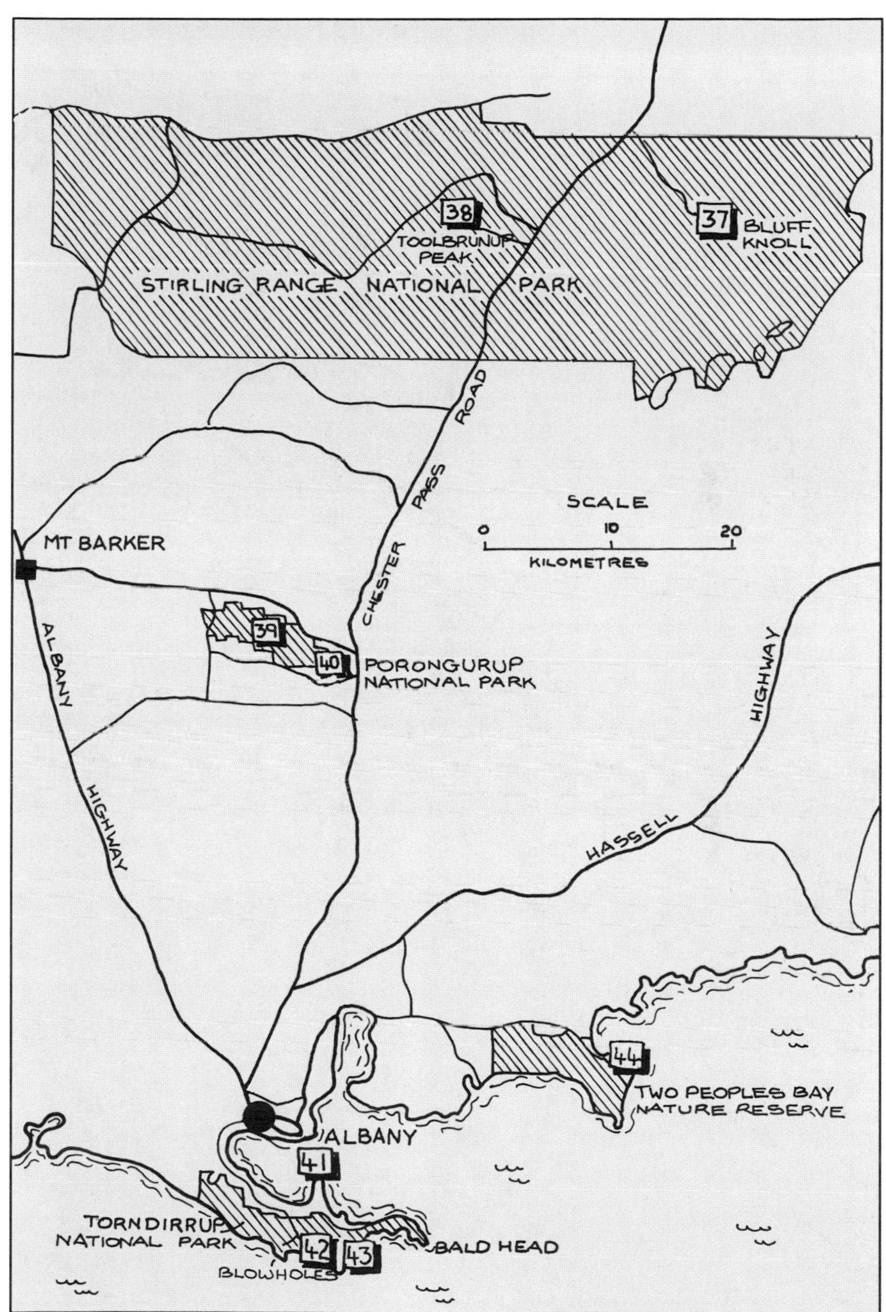

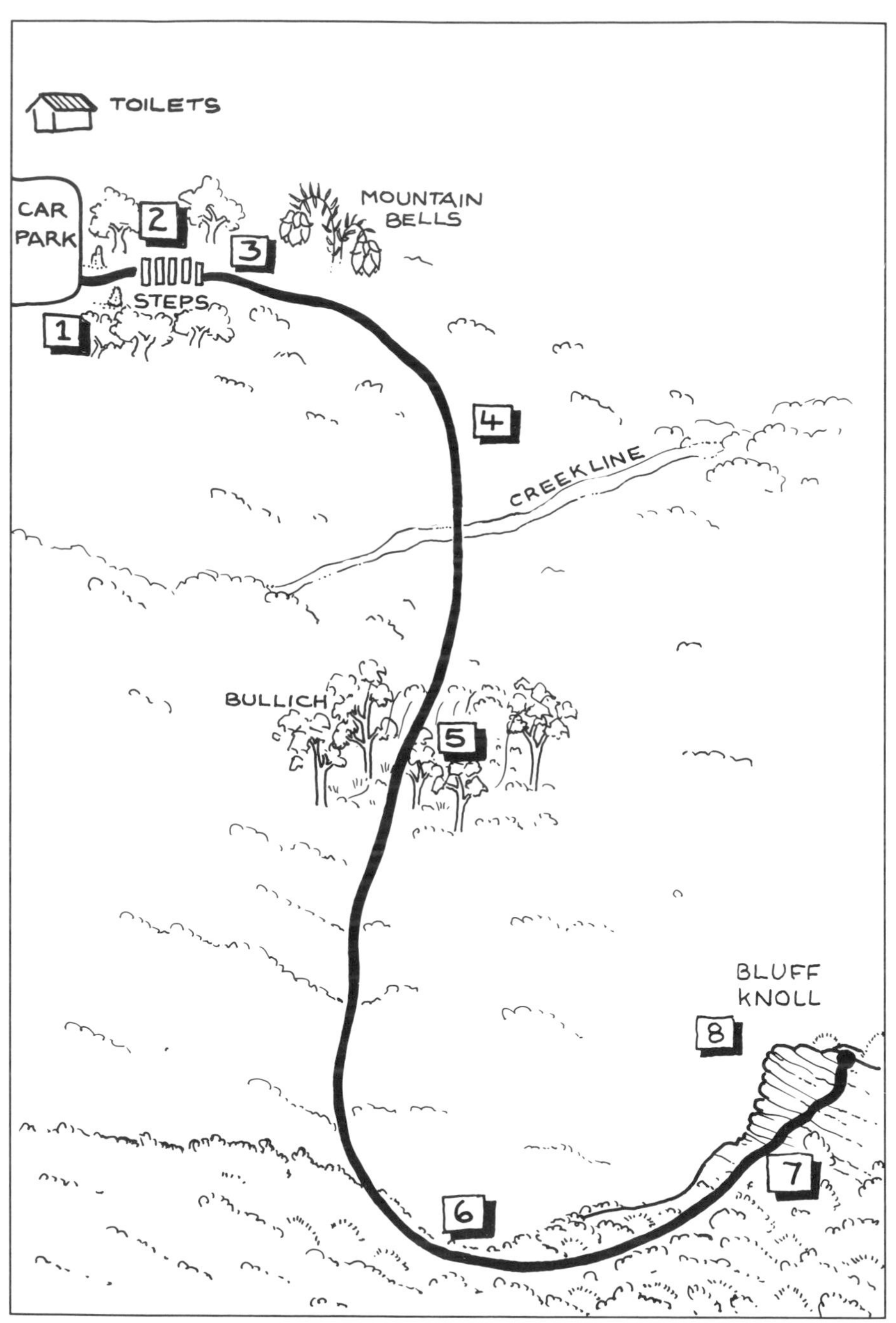
TOILETS
CAR PARK
2
3
MOUNTAIN BELLS
STEPS
1
4
CREEKLINE
BULLICH
5
BLUFF KNOLL
8
7
6

Bluff Knoll

37

Stirling Range National Park

Length: *5 km return.*
Grade: *4. Not recommended in wet or windy conditions or in extreme heat.*
Walk time: *3-4 hours return.*

At 1075 metres, Bluff Knoll is the tallest peak in the South-West of WA. The walk to the summit is straightforward but strenuous. The Stirling Range is renowned for its flora and the Bluff Knoll walk is a good place to view many plants that are only found in the unique conditions provided by the Range. Make sure you carry plenty of drinking water and wear sturdy footwear.

1. The elevation of the range, and the cold air that frequently flows in from the Southern Ocean, mean that Bluff Knoll often experiences unusual weather conditions. The car park is a good place to view cloud formations around the peak. The cloud often streams over the Bluff and descends on the lower gullies. Walkers should always be prepared for a cool change and low cloud. Even on a very hot day you can get a sudden change, with the cool sea breezes coming in. It is advisable to carry warm clothes and a water bottle with you on the walk.
2. Proceed along the path until you reach the first set of steps. Stunted marri and jarrah trees grow near the track. Termite mounds can be seen along the path. Scratches seen in the soil along their sides are a sign that animals, such as Rosenberg's monitors or echidnas, have been searching for a termite meal. Termites have contributed to the soil profile of the Range. The termites bring sand to the surface to build their mounds, separating sand and some mud from the soil beneath.
3. About 100 metres along the path, you can see one of the famed mountain bells. The common mountain bell (*Darwinia lejostyla*) grows on Bluff Knoll. The bells are not true flowers but, in fact, a cluster of flowers that hang down and are enclosed by colourful petal-like leaves referred to as bracts. The common mountain bell has dark pink flowers and is found only in the eastern part of the range. However, it has paler bracts in the valleys below Bluff Knoll compared with bells growing on the summit. Bluff Knoll, like the other peaks of the Range, is a sandstone formation (unlike the nearby Porongurup Range, which is granite). Look up to see the distinctive shape of the peak. The basement geology strongly determines the large landforms within the Range. Thick outcrops of sandstone on quartzite, which dominate the lower and upper parts of the Stirling

Range Formation, are more resistant to weathering and erosion than the middle part, and tend to form the sharp crests and jagged peaks and bluffs.

4. Continue to the creek line. The helmet orchid (*Corybas recurvus*) is seen in cool, damp areas along seasonal creeklines in winter. Once fertilised, this species undergoes an amazing transformation. The tiny, ground-hugging flowers are pushed skywards for up to 30 centimetres by their elongating stem, resulting in the seed being dispersed more effectively by the wind.
5. When you reach the third gully, look for the bullich (*Eucalyptus megacarpa*). This tree looks like a miniature version of the giant karri. Its slender branches are straight or curve smoothly upwards, and the foliage of its open canopy is concentrated into tight clumps at the ends of the branches. It likes swamps and other moist places.
6. From the saddle, you can gain spectacular views of the coast on a clear day, including Bald Island, Two Peoples Bay and Mount Manypeaks. There are permanent wetlands around the saddle (the pass between Bluff Knoll and Coyanarup Peak). Here, you can often hear the croaking of various frog species - the slender tree frog in summer and the small ground frog species during the winter. These areas are also regular haunts of snakes.
7. The path eventually reaches the final summit plateau of Bluff Knoll. Please take care near the cliff edge and watch for the right turn near the final approach to the summit.
8. From the summit you can get a clear view of the Range and the land around it. Note that the eastern peaks are generally higher than those to the west. Mount Success lies just to the west. Toolbrunup Peak, which is only 21 metres lower than Bluff Knoll, is the large conical peak to the west. Mount Hassell lies just to the right of Toolbrunup and Mount Trio is near the park's northern boundary.

Where is it? *The park is about 100 km north-east of Albany via Chester Pass Road.*
Travelling time: *Just over one hour from Albany.*
Facilities: *Tables, toilets and car park.*
Best season: *Spring for wildflowers.*

Allan Rose, Carolyn Thomson and John Watson

MOUNTAIN BELLS

The mountain bells (a group of *Darwinia* species) are perhaps the most famous of the wildflowers found in the Stirling Range. Of the nine species of mountain bell, only the rare Mogumber bell (*Darwinia carnea*) is found outside the Stirling Range. All the bells are closely related, but they are rarely found together, being separated either geographically or by altitude.

All of the mountain bells are pollinated by nectar-feeding birds such as honeyeaters. The pendulous bell appears to be a single flower, but is actually a cluster of small flowers enclosed by colourful petal-like leaves, referred to as bracts.

The Cranbrook bell (*D. meeboldii*) is the emblem of the Cranbrook Shire and grows on the Hamilla Hills and the far western margin of the Range. The tulip darwinia (*D. macrostegia*) has large bells with red veins. It prefers the high, wet slopes of the larger western peaks. The yellow mountain bell (*D. collina*) is probably the most spectacular. Its large lemon-lime bells are often tinged with red on Bluff Knoll and Coyanerup Peak. The common mountain bell (*D. lejostyla*), though far from common, is the second most widespread and probably the most well known. The mountain form of this species has long bright pink bracts.

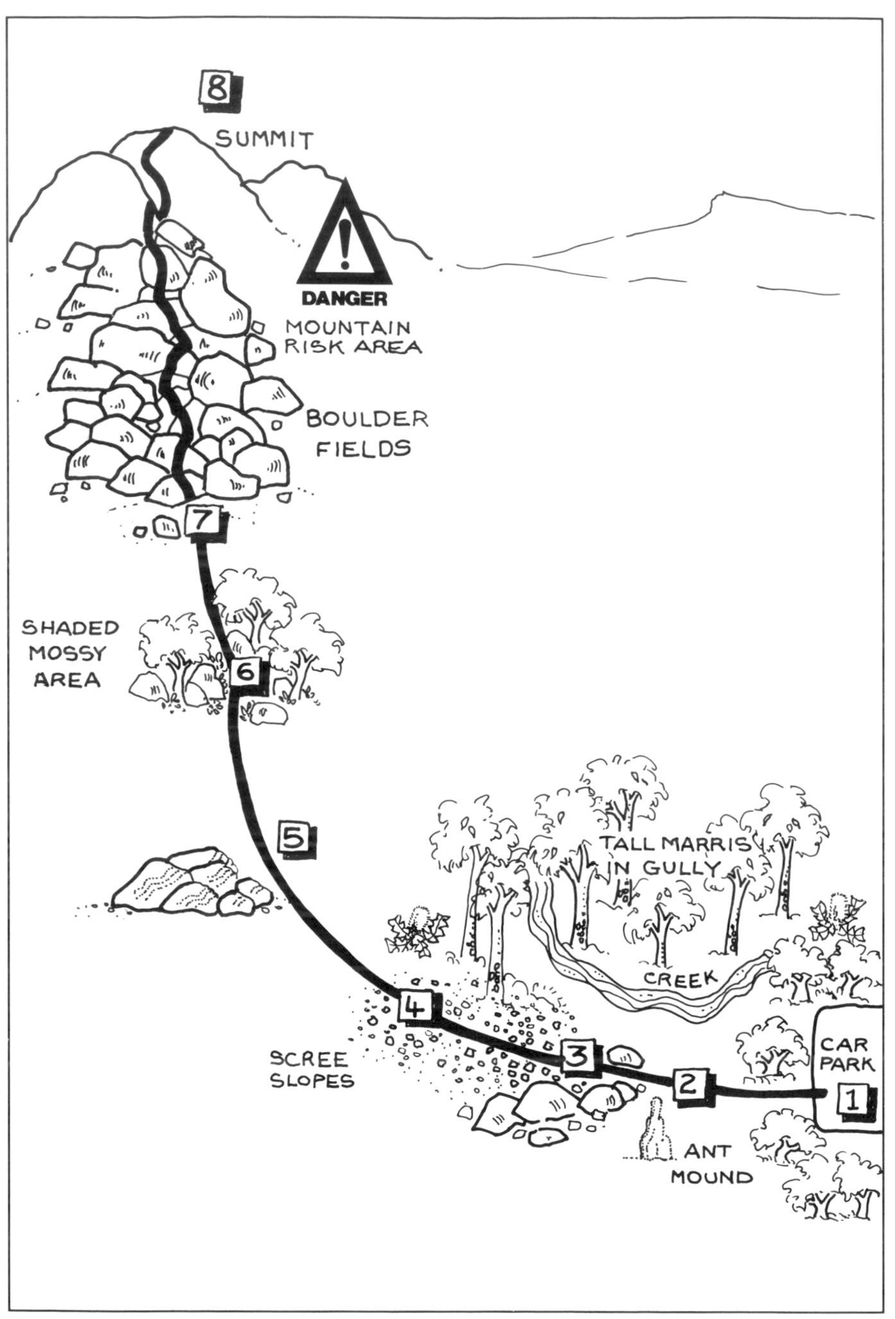
8
SUMMIT
DANGER
MOUNTAIN
RISK AREA
BOULDER
FIELDS
7
SHADED
MOSSY
AREA
6
5
TALL MARRIS
IN GULLY
CREEK
4
SCREE
SLOPES
3
2
CAR
PARK
1
ANT
MOUND

Toolbrunup Peak

38

Stirling Range National Park

Length: *4 km return.*
Grade: *5. Not recommended in wet or windy conditions.*
Walk time: *3-4 hours return.*

Toolbrunup Peak is a more challenging walk than Bluff Knoll, with some rock scrambling towards the top, but the views are worth the effort. Be sure to carry plenty of drinking water and wear sturdy footwear.

1. Woodland of stunted jarrah and marri surrounds the car park. Keep an eye open for golden whistlers and grey shrike-thrushes. In 1832, Ensign Dale visited the Range to find out if kuik and quannet (two types of "grain") grew in the vicinity. Dale scaled Toolbrunup Peak, but failed to find the grain.
2. A large ant mound near the start of the creek marks a good place to look around. The Stirling Range pixie mop (*Isopogon latifolius*) has pink flowers in spring. The white-flowered southern cross is also conspicuous, as it flowers for most of the year. Tiny triggerplants (*Stylidium* species) grow beside the path. There are dense stands of the Stirling Range paper heath (*Sphenotoma* species), whose delicate, papery white flowers scent the valley with honey in spring. The orange flowers in spring are those of large showy dryandra (*Dryandra formosa*). The nectar in these flowers attracts New Holland honeyeaters, which pollinates the plant. Birdwatchers should also watch for white-browed scrub-wrens and white-breasted robins. The creek is fed by run-off from the mountain and the trees are quite large near the creek system. Further back they are much smaller. In places, erosion of the creek bank has exposed river pebbles and creek sediments. The Stirling Range banksia (*Banksia solandri*) can be seen growing on the opposite bank. This plant was first recorded by colonial botanist James Drummond, which he described as having large leaves "irregularly jagged and serrated like an English oak".
3. An open, rocky area is a good spot for lizards basking in the sun. Examine the lichens growing on the rocks. Lichens are composed of an alga (green or bluish-green) and a fungus growing as a co-operative unit. About 30 metres on is a large rock scree. If you pick up some of the rocks you may see the different layers, indicating that these rocks were deposited as beds of sediment. Dainty orchids, such as donkey, slipper and sun orchids, can be spotted in this area. From October to November, the exquisite flowers of the butterfly orchid (*Caladenia*

lobata) show through the accompanying shrubs. For the next 150 metres, amongst the rocky scree, are some of the largest trees (marris) in the park. White-tailed black-cockatoos inhabit this area, probably nesting in tree hollows. Karri hazel, the tall shrubs with broad, soft leaves, grow in the creek. This plant is largely confined to the wetter South-West, but also occurs as an outlier in the creeks of the park.

4. Stop for awhile in a large rock scree overlooking a valley and admire sweeping views of Yungermere Peak. This isolated peak has radiating drainage lines, some of which run into salt lake and swamp country to the south.
5. Pronounced ripple marks in the siltstone rocks show evidence of the sedimentary origin of the Range. Silvereyes can be heard. The red-eared firetail, a specially protected finch species that is rarely seen, is also known from this area.
6. A few metres on is a damp, shaded rocky area covered with mosses and ferns in winter and spring. This has a microclimate of its own - you can actually feel the temperature drop. In winter, stop and search for midge (*Cyrtostylis huegelii*), mosquito (*Cyrtostylis robusta*), and helmet orchids. In summer, the endemic flannel flower (*Actinotus rhomboideus*), with its masses of white pompoms, and a rose-flowered triggerplant with bluish-grey leaves are found here. Both grow only on Toolbrunup Peak and the Bluff Knoll plateau, and both were seen here by Drummond in 1847.
7. A sign warns walkers to proceed with caution beyond this point. From now on you have to clamber over rocks and boulders. Look for the yellow-capped markers placed in the rocks to ensure you are following the correct route.
8. There are spectacular panoramic views from the summit. Pick out the distinctive shapes of Bluff Knoll and the other peaks. To the north are salt lakes and to the south lies the Porongurup Range. Take care to follow the markers on your return from the summit.

Where is it? *The park is about 100 km north-east of Albany via Chester Pass Road.*
Travelling time: *Just under one hour from Albany.*
Facilities: *None at start of trail. Barbecues, tables, toilets, picnic areas and campsites at nearby Moingup Springs.*
Best season: *Spring for wildflowers. This is one of the more sheltered walks in the park and can be undertaken in reasonably warm conditions.*

Carolyn Thomson, Allan Rose and Ian Herford

QUOKKA

Quokkas (*Setonix brachyurus*) were one of the first Australian mammals seen by Europeans. In 1658 Dutch mariner Samuel Volckertzoon wrote of sighting "a wild cat" on Rottnest Island. De Vlamingh thought they were a kind of rat and hence named the island "Rottenest" (Dutch for "rat nest") in 1696. They can be recognised by their rounded bodies with a short tail and a hunched posture. They have small rounded ears and a wide face that is much more flattened than that of other wallabies.

Once very common in areas such as the Swan Coastal Plain near Perth and Gingin, quokkas are now uncommon on the mainland and are confined to isolated pockets within the south-west corner of WA. They are, however, found at Dwellingup, Jarrahdale, Harvey, Collie (near Wellington Dam), in Stirling Range National Park and along the South Coast to Two Peoples Bay. On the mainland, densely vegetated areas around swamps or streams are preferred. Quokkas occur in large numbers on Rottnest Island, near Perth, and Bald Island, east of Albany, where they inhabit low and scrubby vegetation where water is not always available year round.

Their low numbers on the mainland, compared with relatively large numbers in less than optimum habitat on fox-free Rottnest Island, suggest that mainland populations are heavily predated by foxes.

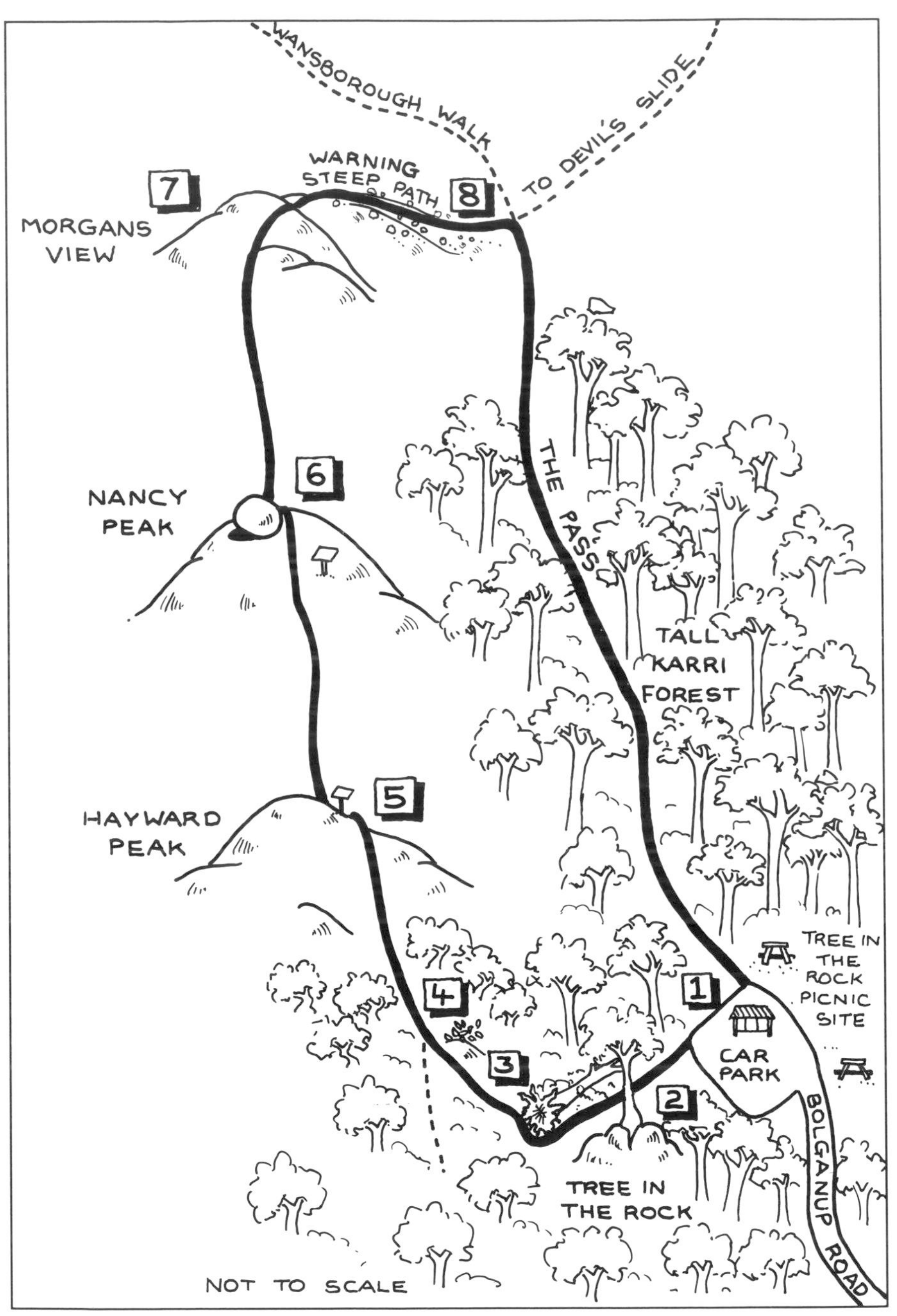
WANSBOROUGH WALK
TO DEVIL'S SLIDE
WARNING
STEEP PATH
7
8
MORGANS
VIEW
THE PASS
6
NANCY
PEAK
TALL
KARRI
FOREST
5
HAYWARD
PEAK
TREE IN
THE
ROCK
PICNIC
SITE
4
1
3
CAR
PARK
2
BOLGANUP ROAD
TREE IN
THE ROCK
NOT TO SCALE

Nancy Peak Loop

39

Porongurup National Park ($)

Length: *5.5 kilometres.*
Grade: *4.*
Walk time: *2-3 hours.*

The Nancy Peak Loop is a strenuous but enjoyable walk up and over three peaks. Ensure you carry plenty of drinking water and wear sturdy footwear.

1. Begin at the information shelter at the Tree in the Rock picnic area. Along the path, moss-covered logs decorate the karri (*Eucalyptus diversicolor*) forest floor, while scarlet and yellow robins, rufous tree-creepers and other birds can usually be seen perched on branches.
2. About 100 metres from the start is the Tree in the Rock, a karri that found a foothold in a crevice and gradually enlarged it as it grew. Karri and marri (*Corymbia calophylla*) are the most dominant trees in this area, while karri hazel (*Trymalium floribundum*), karri wattle (*Acacia pentadenia*), and tassel bush (*Leucopogon verticillatis*) form part of the understorey. Australian bluebell (*Sollya heterophylla*) can be recognised by its small bell-like mauve flowers from October to February.
3. The track climbs sharply upwards and then diverts around a large dead karri which has uprooted, displaying its twisted roots. A little further on, succulent pigface (*Carpobrotus* species) perches on top of a granite outcrop.
4. Passing a small track that veers to the left, you should continue along the main path. Note that the marri and karri are increasingly gnarled and stunted, compared with the tall, straight trees of the picnic area.
5. From Hayward Peak (1.73 km along the walk) you have great views to the Stirling Range. You can also see a dam below. Look for a plaque that gives further information about the peak.
6. The path makes its way downwards and then upwards, to scale Nancy Peak, from which there are stunning vistas southward to Albany. This section covers about 650 metres.
7. It is a further 640 metres to Morgans View, which is considerably lower than Hayward and Nancy Peaks. You can see the aptly named Devil's Slide, a large steeply sloping area of bare and moss-covered granite, to the west. After taking in the views, you will have to clamber down a rocky path that is quite steep, and rocky and loose underfoot, so take great care.
8. After about 600 metres, the path intersects with The Pass. Turn right through

attractive karri forest along the fire access track to return to the picnic area, a further 1.6 km, but mostly downhill.

Where is it? *50 km north of Albany via Chester Pass Road, Porongurup Road and Bolganup Road. 20 km east of Mount Barker via Porongurup Road and Bolganup Road.*
Travelling time: *40 minutes from Albany, 20 minutes from Mount Barker.*
Facilities: *Picnic tables, barbecues and toilets.*
On-site information: *Information display at start of path, interpretive signs and occasional track markers en route.*
Best season: *Spring and early summer for wildflowers. Can be hot and humid in summer and very wet in winter.*

Carolyn Thomson and Peter Dans

AUSTRALIAN BLUEBELL

The Australian bluebell (*Sollya heterophylla*) is a common bushland plant of south-western Australia. The Australian bluebell is easily recognised by its twining habit and its small, intense blue, bell-like flowers up to three millimetres long. It is the most common of the three species of *Sollya*, which are unique to WA.

This small shrub or twiner reaches one and a half metres high. Its leafy stems often twist around themselves and associated plants. Its glossy green, leathery leaves are up to five centimetres long, while the pendulous deep blue flowers are generally arranged in loose inflorescences. Australian bluebell flowers sporadically throughout the year, but mainly from October to February. The flowers mature into fleshy blue berries up to two and a half centimetres long. These are edible when ripe and are quite sweet with a soft texture.

The Australian bluebell is widespread, growing in a variety of habitats in the South-West, from Mogumber to Augusta and east to the Esperance area.

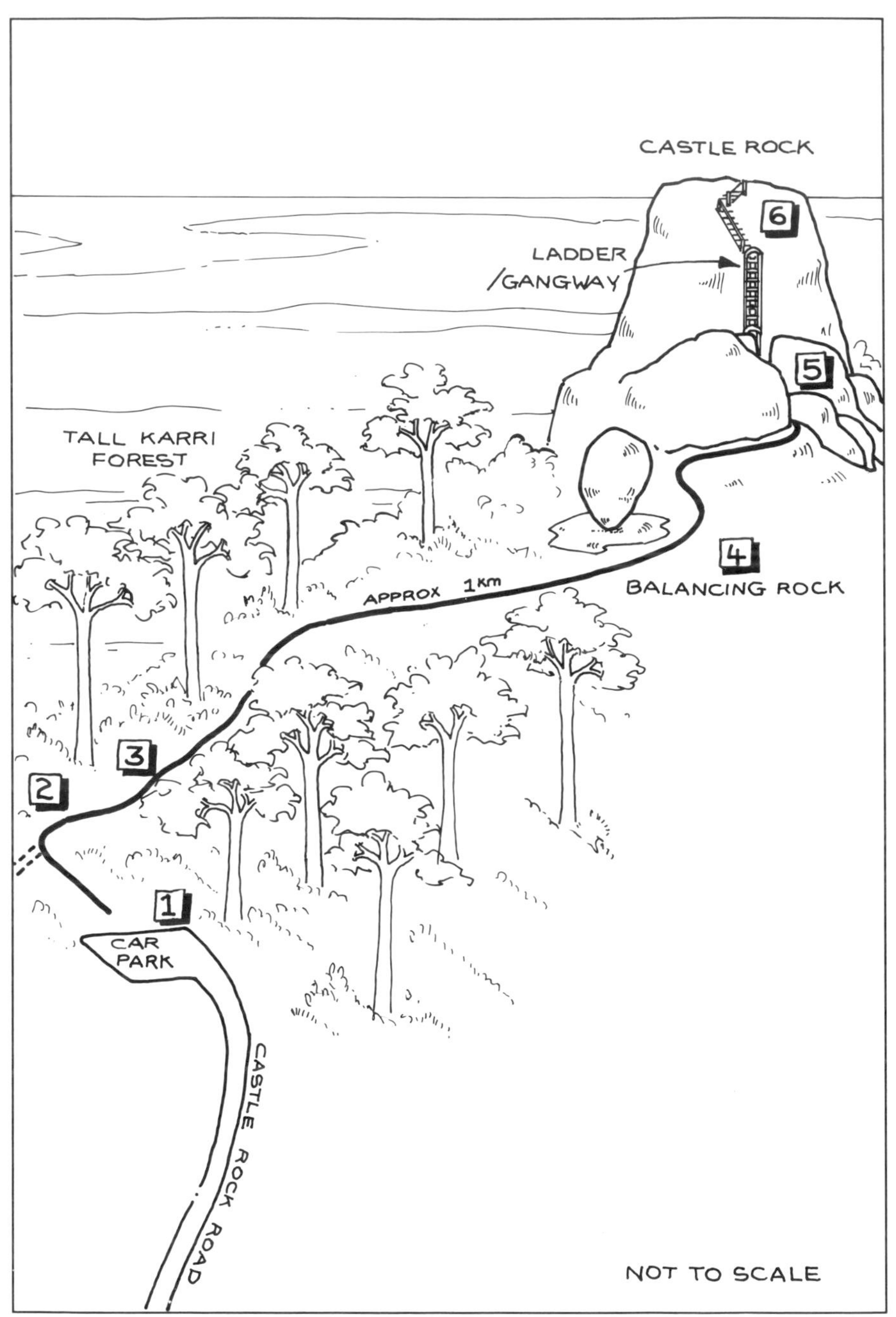
CASTLE ROCK
6
LADDER
/GANGWAY
5
TALL KARRI
FOREST
4
BALANCING ROCK
APPROX 1km
3
2
1
CAR
PARK
CASTLE ROCK ROAD
NOT TO SCALE

Castle Rock

Porongurup National Park ($)

9/1/98

Great views, nice walk easier down than up.

Length: *4 km.*
Grade: *4.*
Walk time: *$1^1/_2$ to 2 hours.*

The Castle Rock walk is a pleasant alternative to the Nancy Peak Circuit. It traverses karri forest and passes the Balancing Rock, before the final steep ascent of Castle Rock via an enclosed ladder and gangway. There are superb views to the south from the summit.

1. Begin at the steps on the southern side of the car park and make your way through some magnificent karri forest.
2. Follow the path before you reach the firebreak, then turn right.
3. Follow the firebreak and then the footpath, gradually ascending.
4. One of the walk's main features is the aptly named Balancing Rock. When granite is well-jointed, it erodes into boulders with a rounded shape. Erosion at their base may lead to precarious-looking balancing rocks like the one before you.
5. Just after the Balancing Rock, scramble up to your right, as indicated by the signs. Go through a narrow cleft in the rocks to the base of the ladder.
6. Follow the ladder and gangway to the 'battlements' of Castle Rock. The granite rocks from which the Porongurup Range is composed are about 1100 million years old. They are thought to be a melted portion of the Australian continental plate, which cooled under intense pressure at least 10 to 12 kilometres below the surface. Erosion of the surrounding softer rocks resulted in the harder granites being exposed as a mountain range. The exposed granites were then eroded to form large, bare, round-topped peaks interspersed with deep valleys.

Where is it? *Approximately 45 km from Albany via Chester Pass Road, Porongurup Road and Castle Rock Road.*
Travelling time: *35 minutes from Albany.*
Facilities: *Car park, picnic table.*
On-site information: *Signs, track markers and an interpretive sign near the summit. There is a plaque on the summit rock.*
Best season: *All year, but it can be hot and humid in summer and very wet in winter.*

John Watson

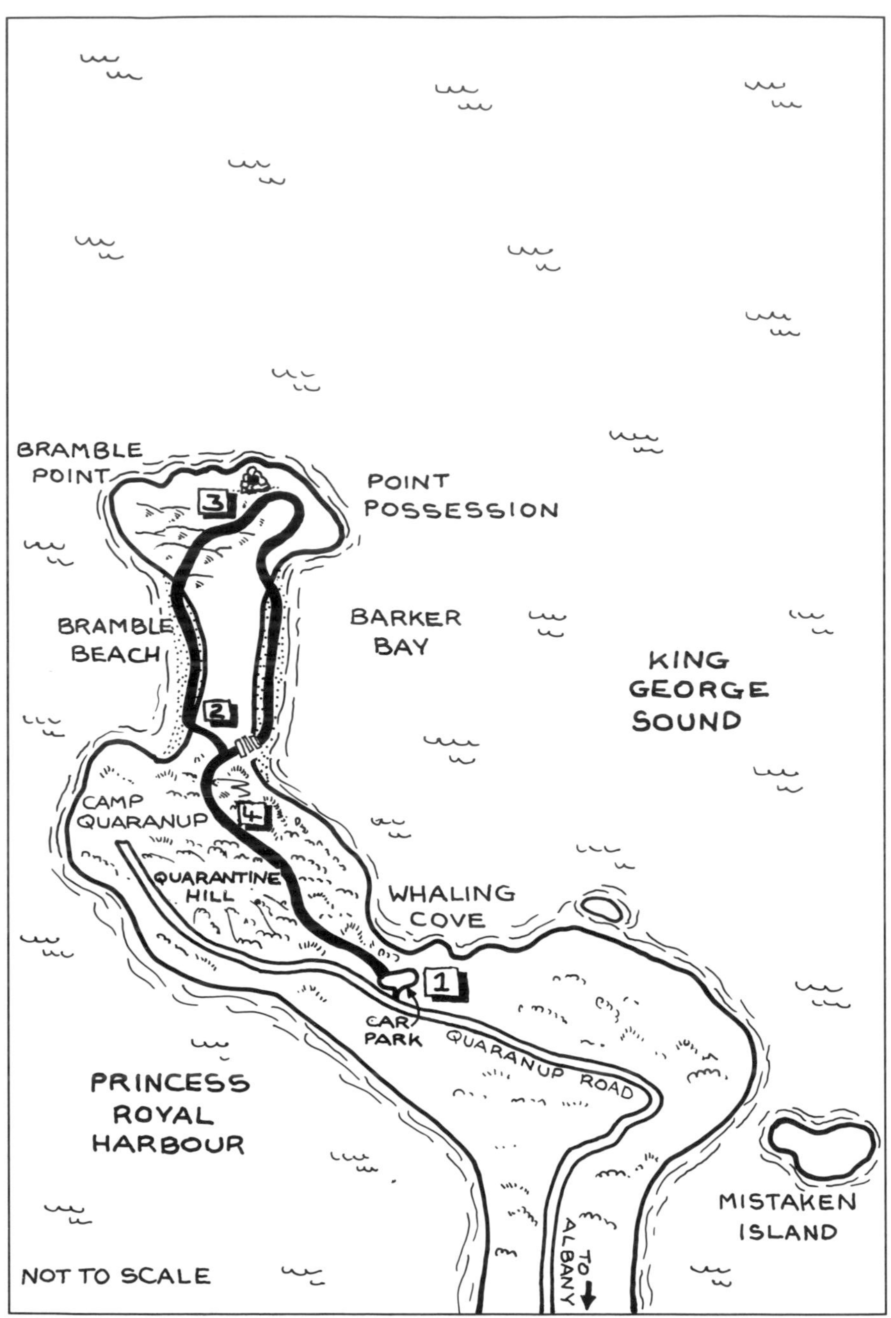
BRAMBLE POINT
POINT POSSESSION
3
BRAMBLE BEACH
BARKER BAY
KING GEORGE SOUND
2
CAMP QUARANUP
4
QUARANTINE HILL
WHALING COVE
1
CAR PARK
QUARANUP ROAD
PRINCESS ROYAL HARBOUR
MISTAKEN ISLAND
TO ALBANY
NOT TO SCALE

Point Possession Heritage Trail

41

Vancouver Peninsula, Albany

Length: *4 km.*
Grade: *4.*
Walk time: *2 hours.*

The Point Possession Heritage Trail is an excellent walk along the northern section of the peninsula via Quarantine Hill, Bramble Beach, Point Possession and returning via Barker Bay. It provides excellent views of Princess Royal Harbour, Albany and King George Sound. A cairn and plaque record the historic landing by George Vancouver in 1791 and there are interpretive plaques along the route.

1. Begin on the western side of the car park and follow the path around the seaward side of Quarantine Hill, through heathlands, low woodland and open granite slabs, before descending to Bramble Bay.
2. Head northwards along Bramble Beach, adjacent to the waters of Princess Royal Harbour, and ascend Point Possession via the marked route over granite rocks.
3. After visiting the cairn, the path meanders around the eastern side of the hill and swings back southward to the north end of Barker Bay Beach. Follow the beach to the southern end, where a short set of steps and an old four-wheel-drive access track lead back to the outward path. Note the marked differences between Bramble Beach and the beach at Barker Bay, which is exposed to the swells of King George Sound.
4. Return by the same route over Quarantine Hill to the car park.

Where is it? *The Shire reserve lies 25 km (by road) south of Albany via Frenchman Bay Road. Turn left along Quaranup Road for 5.5 km to the Whaling Cove car park signposted on the right.*
Travelling time: *30 minutes from Albany.*
Facilities: *Car park.*
On-site information: *Interpretive plaques and path markers.*
Best season: *An excellent walk all year.*

John Watson

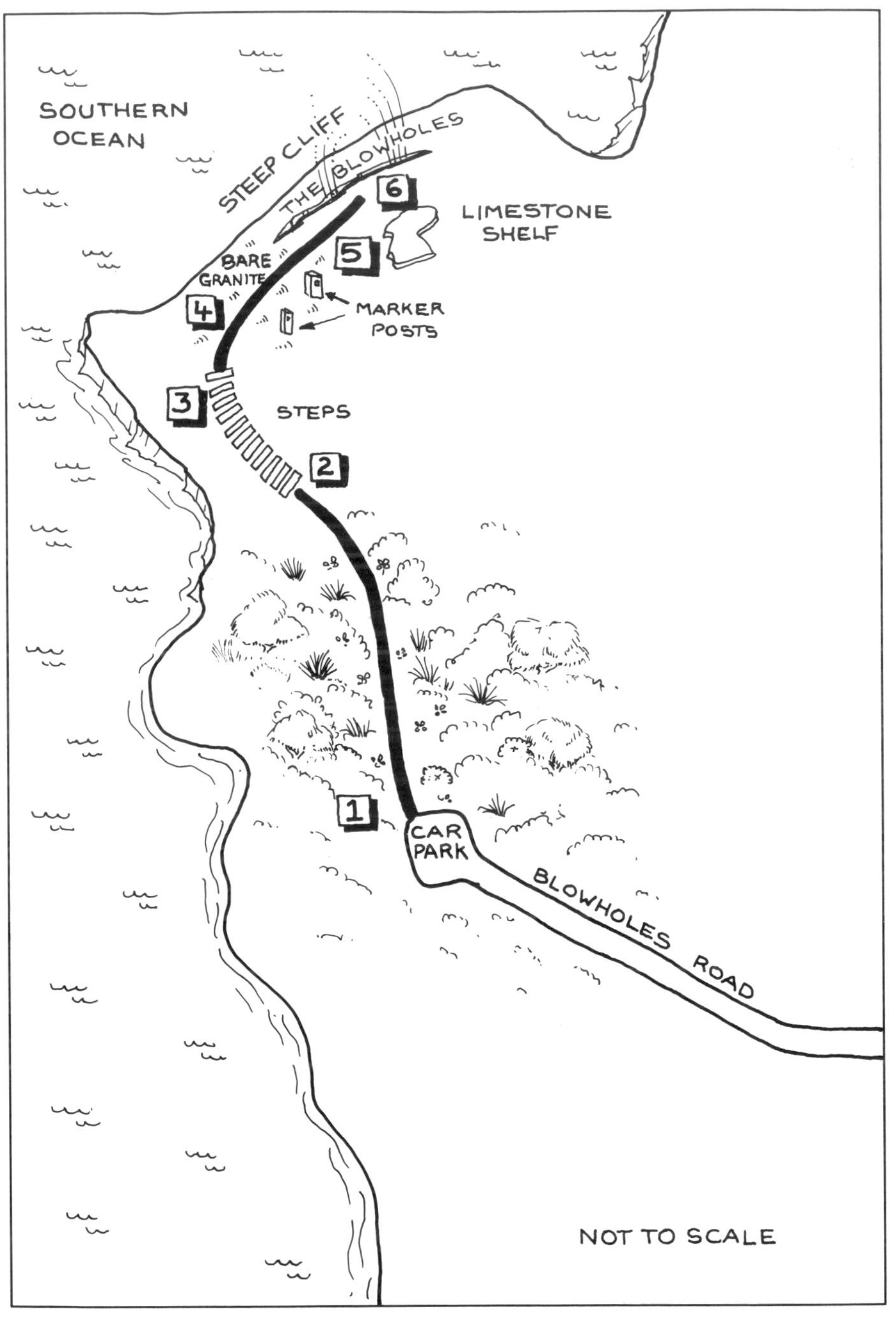
SOUTHERN
OCEAN
STEEP CLIFF
THE BLOWHOLES
6
LIMESTONE
SHELF
5
BARE
GRANITE
4
MARKER
POSTS
3
STEPS
2
1
CAR
PARK
BLOWHOLES ROAD
NOT TO SCALE

The Blowholes

Torndirrup National Park

Length: *1.6 km return.*
Grade: *1.*
Walk time: *50 minutes.*

Albany's Blowholes should not be missed, especially on a day when the ocean swell is high. This walk is the most popular in Torndirrup National Park. Keep away from the ocean at all times, as several lives have been lost in this vicinity.

1. The path begins at the western end of the car park and is well signposted. It passes through some interesting coastal vegetation, including coastal banjine (*Pimelia ferruginea*), recognised by its heads of pink flowers. The shrubs with a woolly appearance and small, intensely red flowers are woollybush (*Adenanthos* species) while basketbush (*Spiridium globulosum*) has oval leaves that are dark green above and very pale beneath. Coastal sword sedge (*Lepidosperma gladiatum*), peppermints (*Agonis flexuosa*), thick-leaved fanflower (*Scaevola crassifolia*), buttercups (*Hibbertia* species), various banksias and native rosemary (*Olearia axillaris*) can also be seen. See how many species you can recognise.
2. Follow the gravel path for about 400 metres to the top of the steps. There are fine views of Peak Head to the south-east and Eclipse Island to the south-west.
3. Continue down the steps when the path swings to the right.
4. After negotiating an open granite area, follow the large track markers and sections of formed footpath.
5. Signs indicate the locations of the Blowholes, a crackline in the granite that "blows" air and occasionally spray. The noise is quite impressive.
6. Cross to the Blowholes but do not proceed any further towards the ocean and do not stand over the Blowholes. Here, visitors can see all of the park's major rock types in close proximity. People often sit on a shelf of light-coloured rock to observe the spray. This 'seat' is composed of limestone, formed from sand dunes 120 000 years ago. While sitting on the limestone, visitors dangle their feet onto the darker rocks below. These are the granites, almost 1200 million years old, which once glued Antarctica to Australia. Embedded in the granites are rounded darker patches of rock. These are the gneisses, which formed part of the Australian and Antarctic continents before the formation of the supercontinent Gondwana and extend the story back between 1300 and 1600 million years.
7. Return to the car park by the same route.

Where is it? *The park is 18 km south of Albany via Frenchman Bay Road and Blowholes Road.*
Travelling time: *20 minutes from Albany.*
Facilities: *Car park - please do not leave valuables in your vehicle.*
On-site information: *Coastal safety advice, path markers along the route.*
Best season: *All year, especially when a high ocean swell is running.*

John Watson

ALBANY PITCHER PLANT

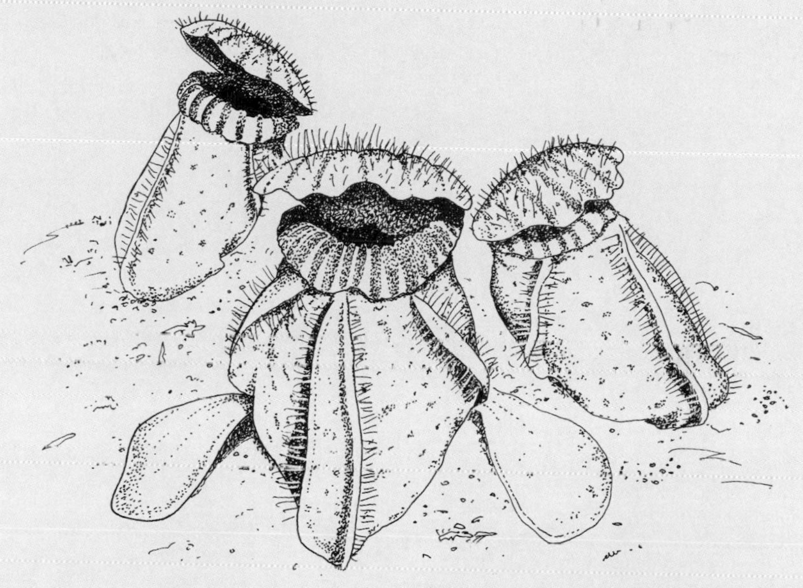

The Albany pitcher plant *(Cephalotus follicularis)* contains a deadly trap. The sack-like pitchers, which are modified leaves, hold a watery fluid which attracts insects. While attempting to feed, the insect slides down the shiny ribs on the mouth of the pitcher and into the fluid. The pitcher's smooth, overhanging walls, and its ring of downward-pointing teeth, thwarts any escape. The insect then drowns and decomposes to provide nourishment for the plant. The lid of the pitcher is not part of the trap, but may protect the liquid from excessive evaporation.

The Albany pitcher plant is the sole member of its family. It is often hidden in the dense vegetation fringing swamps and creeks, in scattered localities between Augusta and Cheyne Beach, near Albany.

This small, perennial herb has two types of leaves, which form a basal rosette. The thick, flat innermost leaves are between 10 and 50 millimetres long. The outermost leaves are modified into pitchers, which are green in the shade but tinged with red or purple when growing in sunlight. The pitchers, up to five and a half centimetres high, are topped with a lid which rises, as the pitcher matures, to reveal the strongly ribbed opening.

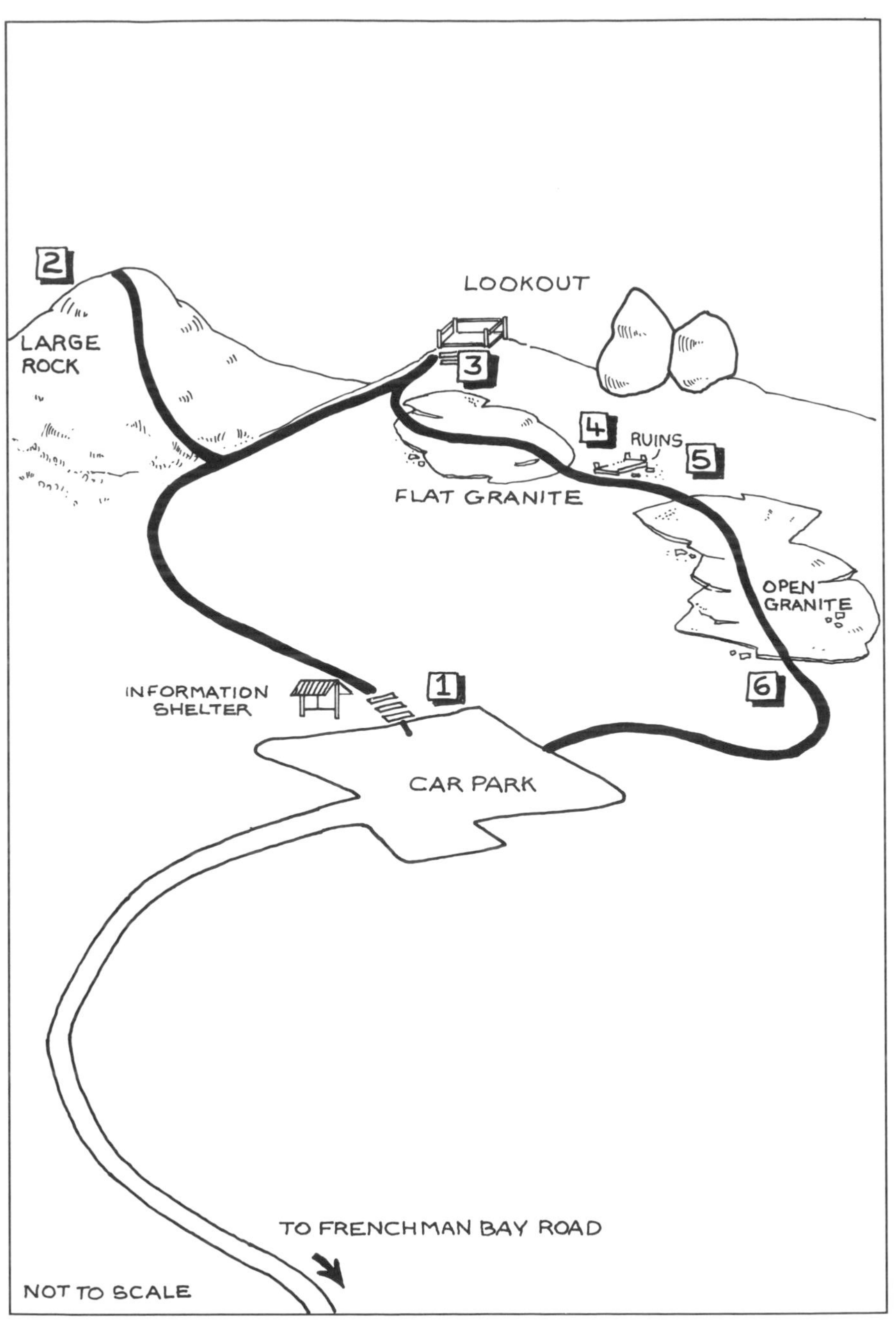
2
LARGE ROCK
LOOKOUT
3
4
RUINS
5
FLAT GRANITE
OPEN GRANITE
INFORMATION SHELTER
1
6
CAR PARK
TO FRENCHMAN BAY ROAD
NOT TO SCALE

Stony Hill

43

Torndirrup National Park

9/1/98

Excellent short walk w/c interesting vegetation.

Length: *400 metre circuit.*
Grade: *1.*
Walk time: *20 minutes.*

This short walk provides a spectacular scenic circuit of the highest point in Torndirrup National Park. The path is part of the Western Australian Heritage Trails Network established as a Bicentennial Commemorative Program in 1988. Interpretive plaques along the trail describe some of the thoughts and feelings experienced by the first settlers to this area. There are magnificent views of Albany, King George Sound, Eclipse Island, West Cape Howe and the Porongurup and Stirling ranges.

1. The heritage trail begins at the steps on the southern side of the car park. Read about some of Albany's early history at the information display.
2. Follow the limestone path until a large granite rock beckons on the left. Here you have the option of climbing to the summit of the rock, but if you do so please take care, as the surface can be quite slippery.
3. Continue to follow the limestone path and proceed to the wooden lookout for views to the west.
4. Follow the track markers across flat granite rocks, then pick up the continuation of the limestone path and pass the nearby ruins of an old radar station.
5. As the path swings towards the north, a magnificent view back to Albany and the Stirling Range unfolds.
6. Cross over more slabs of open granite, following the markers to the next section of limestone path. Follow the path back to the car park.

Where is it? *20 km south of Albany via Frenchman Bay Road and Stony Hill Road.*
Travelling time: *20 minutes from Albany.*
Facilities: *Interpretive plaques, lookout platform. Toilets and refreshments at Frenchmans Bay, 5 minutes drive away.*
On-site information: *Information display at start, interpretive plaques and track markers along the route.*
Best season: *All year - a great introduction to Torndirrup National Park, with 360° views of the Albany area.*

John Watson

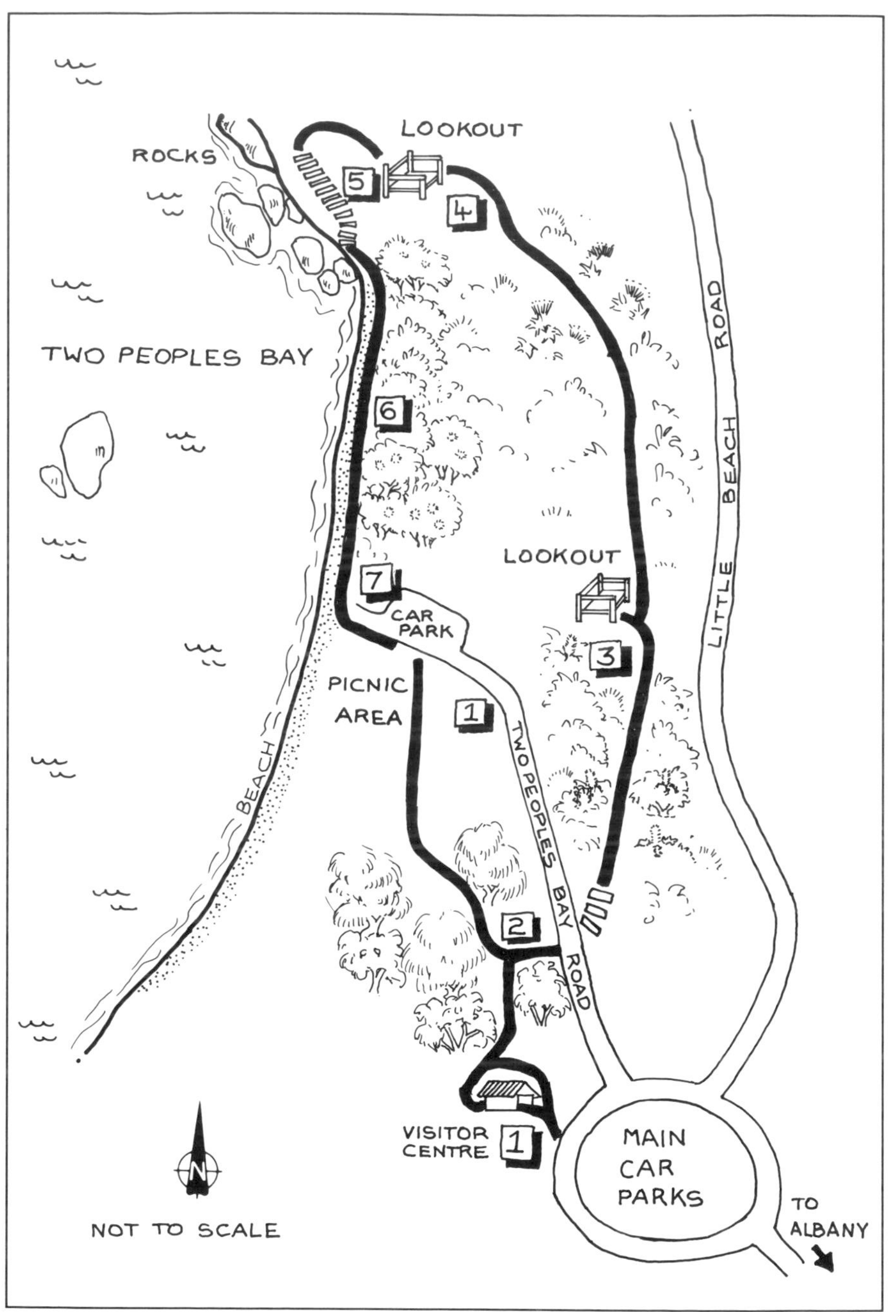
LOOKOUT
ROCKS
5
4
TWO PEOPLES BAY
6
LITTLE BEACH ROAD
LOOKOUT
7
CAR PARK
3
PICNIC AREA
1
TWO PEOPLES BAY ROAD
BEACH
2
VISITOR CENTRE
1
MAIN CAR PARKS
N
NOT TO SCALE
TO ALBANY

Baie Des Deux Peuples Heritage Trail

44

Two Peoples Bay Nature Reserve

Length: *2 km return.*
Grade: *1.*
Walk time: *1 hour.*

The heritage trail provides an excellent introduction to Two Peoples Bay Nature Reserve, home of the Gilbert's potoroo, the noisy scrub-bird and several other threatened animal species. Two lookouts provide views of Mount Manypeaks across the bay and the lake systems of the nature reserve, with the Porongurup and Stirling ranges visible on a clear day. The walk returns along the beach. Noisy scrub-birds may sometimes be heard in the area. The starting point for this path is being redesigned and a linking path is being established to Little Beach.

1. You may start this walk from either the visitor centre car park or from the information display in the picnic area closer to the beach. In either case the new paths are clearly marked.
2. The two approach routes join the edge of the peppermint, bullich and yate woodland, from where you cross the main road, being watchful for cars, and climb the steps.
3. Follow the limestone path, through an area inhabited by stunted banksias, to the first lookout, which provides delightful views over the bay.
4. Retrace your steps for five metres then take the left branch and follow a narrower path until you reach the second lookout. See if you can recognise parrotbush (*Dryandra sessilis*) and prostrate hakea (*Hakea prostrata*), while you listen for the musical calls of the noisy scrub-bird.
5. Descend down steep steps to the sea. Diggings around the steps are very noticeable and are the handiwork of the southern brown bandicoot, one of a number of endangered species which inhabit the reserve. Explore around the boulders, where Kings skinks shelter in crevices. In summer this would make an excellent area for snorkelling.
6. Return to the car park by heading back along the seagrass (*Posidonia australis*) covered beach. Watch out for snakes here and avoid soft patches of seaweed if you want to keep your feet dry. Dense thickets of one-eyed wattle (*Acacia cyclops*) fringe the beach. Examine the seed pods. Each seed is circled by a bright red stalk that resembles a bloodshot eye. Sea rocket (*Cakile maritima*), an introduced species with mauve flowers, has colonised the sandy beach itself. You can sometimes see large Pacific gulls resting on the beach.

7. Turn left at the road and return to the picnic area (50 metres), from where you may continue to the visitor centre (250 metres).

Where is it? *40 km east of Albany via Lower King Road, Nanarup Road and Two Peoples Bay Road.*
Travelling time: *40 minutes from Albany.*
Facilities: *Car park, barbecues, toilets, benches along route, lookouts.*
On-site information: *Visitor centre and information display. Some track markers along route.*
Best season: *All year.*

John Watson

GILBERT'S POTOROO

In one of the most exciting biological finds of the decade, Gilbert's potoroo (*Potorous tridactylus gilbertii*) was rediscovered by zoology students in November 1994 at Two Peoples Bay Nature Reserve. This primitive relation of kangaroos and wallabies was last recorded some time between 1874 and 1879 and thought to be extinct.

The potoroo has quite a round face. Its ears are almost buried in the long, soft fur that covers its whole body, but its eyes provide clear vision of things above and in front, and its front feet are armed with powerful claws for digging. The tail is longer and stouter than that of a bandicoot. Gilbert's potoroos dig small holes to obtain truffles (underground fungi), which probably form the bulk of their diet. They are largely nocturnal but begin to feed at dusk.

Gilbert's potoroo, which was known to Aboriginal people as ngil-gyte, is believed to be a subspecies of the long-nosed potoroo of south-eastern Australia. The Department of Conservation and Land Management is closely monitoring the single population and undertaking fox control to protect it. Research into the animal's conservation needs is underway. Scientists have now embarked on a search for new populations elsewhere.

The Vast South-East Walks 45 - 49

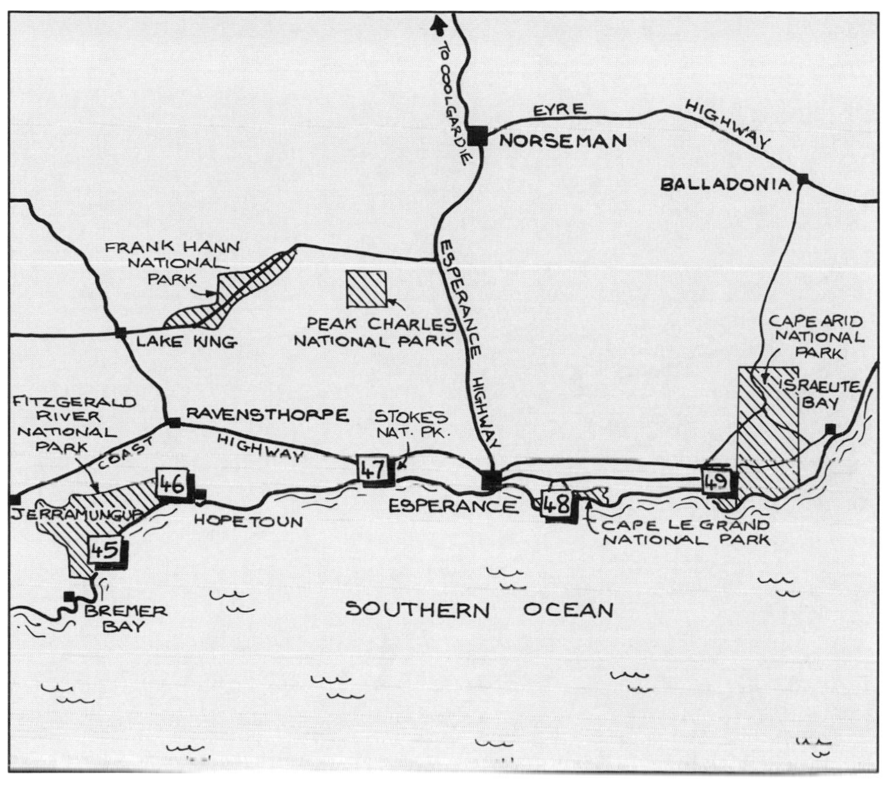

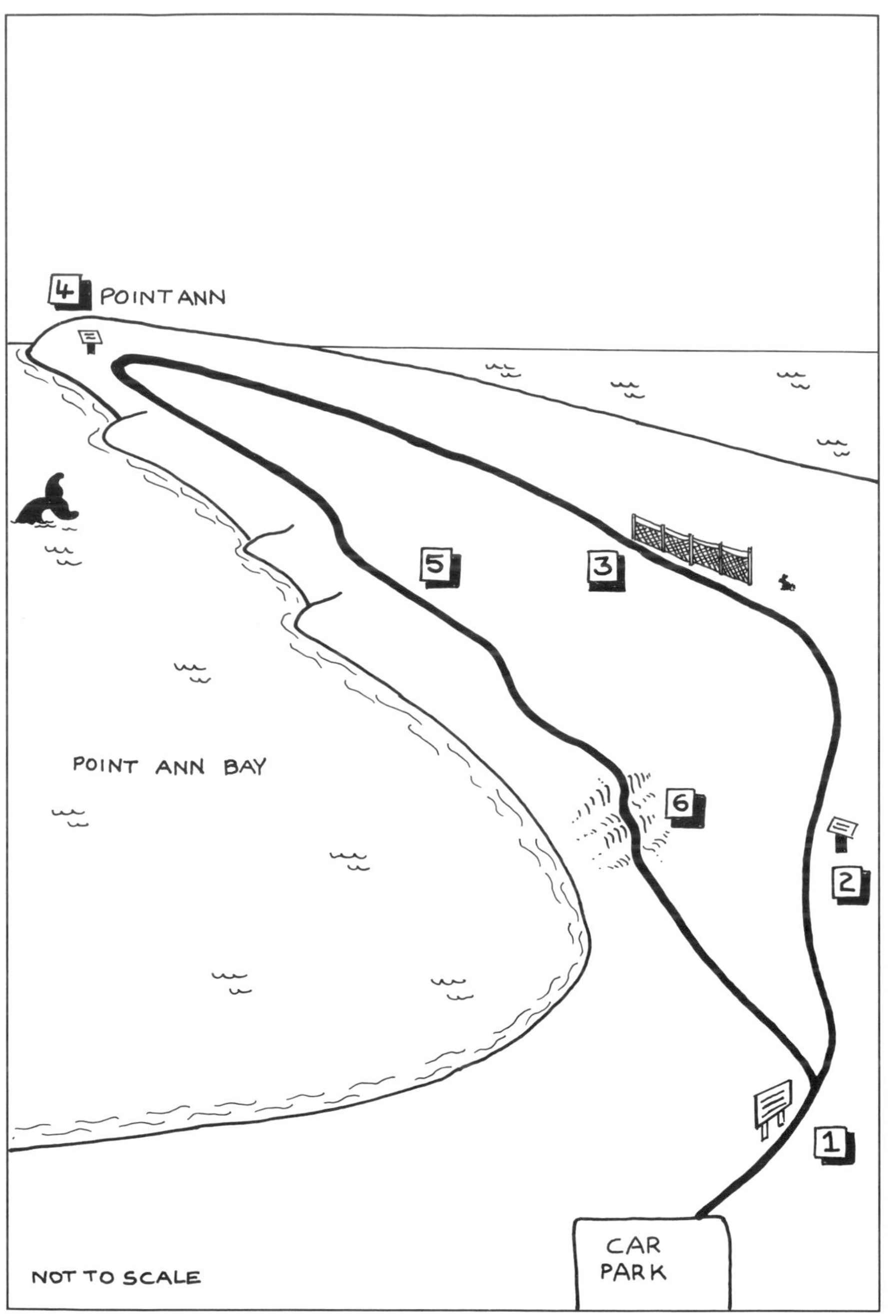
4 POINT ANN
5
3
6
2
1
POINT ANN BAY
CAR PARK
NOT TO SCALE

Point Ann Heritage Trail

45

Fitzgerald River National Park

Length: *1.5 km circuit.*
Grade: *1.*
Walk time: *45 minutes.*

This walk is a pleasant circuit of Point Ann. Plaques along the way focus on the history of the Rabbit Proof Fence and the whales which are frequently visible from July to October.

1. Start at the Heritage Trail sign. Please clean your footwear using the boot cleaning station provided, to minimise the risk of inadvertently spreading the plant-killing *Phytophthora* dieback via infected soil on your shoes.
2. After 10 metres, follow the right hand branch of the trail, which is along one wheel way of an old four-wheel-drive track. After a few hundred metres you will join the fence line proper, where another disused track comes in from your right.
3. A short distance beyond, you will reach a section of the old Rabbit Proof Fence which has been retained. The plaques tell the intriguing story about this "longest single fence in the world".
4. Continue to the headland terminus where you stand with ocean on 270°, as on the bridge or prow of a ship. Watch and listen for whales at this point. Note also how the vegetation is heavily 'wind pruned' in this vicinity. Plants which would normally be up to two metres high rarely attain 0.5 - 1 metres in height here.
5. The path heads back via the north side of the headland, towards the car park and Point Ann beach. Across the bay there are magnificent views of the Mid Mt Barren and Thumb Peak mountain ranges in the central wilderness area of this world renowned national park.
6. After crossing two small gullies, the path returns to the starting point.

Where is it? *About 55 km east of Bremer Bay via Swamp Rd, Devils Creek Rd, Pabelup Dve and Point Ann Rd.*
Travelling time: *2 1/2 hours from Albany, 1 hour from Bremer Bay.*
Facilities: *Picnic shelters and toilets at Point Ann, camping facilities at St Marys (1 km). Boot cleaning station at start of walk.*
On-site information: *Interpretive plaques along the way and trail markers.*
Best season: *All year but whales most likely July-October.*

John Watson

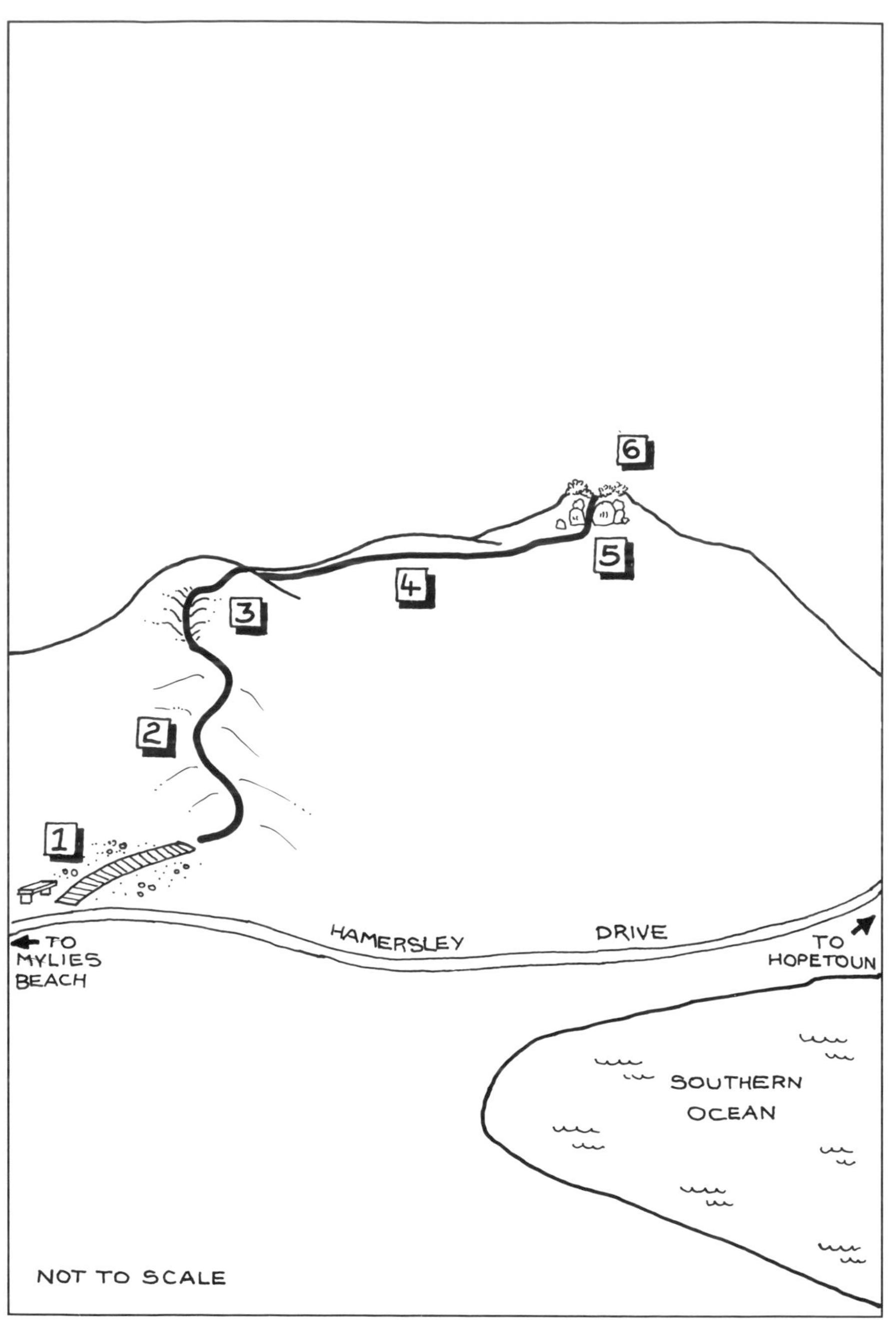
6
5
4
3
2
1
TO MYLIES BEACH
HAMERSLEY
DRIVE
TO HOPETOUN
SOUTHERN OCEAN
NOT TO SCALE

East Mount Barren

46

Fitzgerald River National Park

Length: *3 km return.*
Grade: *4.*
Walk time: *2-3 hours.*

East Mt Barren is located at the eastern end of the renowned Fitzgerald River National Park. The Barrens (West, Mid and East) were named by Matthew Flinders as he sailed along the coast in the *Investigator* in January 1802. Far from being 'barren', these hills are covered with vegetation, which is among the most unique and diverse in WA.

An interpretive brochure which describes several of these species is available on site at the start of the walk.

1. Follow the boardwalk across an old gravel pit infected with the plant-killing dieback (*Phytophthora*) disease. Please scrub down your footwear at the boot cleaning station and stay on the boardwalk. This will minimise the risk of spreading dieback disease further upslope.
2. Follow the path as it meanders up a low quartzite ridge. In season, you will pass through magnificent stands of Barrens regelia (*Regelia velutina*), which has crimson flowers atop majestic pale green stems.
3. The ridge ahead is quite steep for about 150 metres. At first, the path heads up a gully slightly to the left, then it turns onto the spine of the ridge. If it is wet or windy please be doubly careful on this section, which is the steepest and generally the most exposed to the elements on the walk.
4. Follow the path along the gently sloping ridge, then head up again and through a narrow gap in the ridge to the final saddle before the summit peak.
5. From afar the route to the summit appears problematical, but the path winds up between steep boulders and small rock faces to emerge on a small bushy saddle.
6. The end of the path is a few metres to the left, next to the cairn of stones.
7. Return to the start of the walk by the same path.

The view from the top of East Mount Barren and for much of the descent is spectacular. On a clear day, you can see most of the peaks of the Fitzgerald River National Park and the Doubtful Islands, some 65 kilometres to the south-west. The westernmost islands of the Recherche Archipelago, near Esperance, are visible in really good conditions.

Where is it? *10 km west of Hopetoun via Southern Ocean West Road and Hamersley Drive.*
Travelling time: *15 minutes from Hopetoun.*
Facilities: *Boardwalk and boot cleaning station at commencement.*
On-site information: *Interpretive brochure on site plus track markers along the way.*
Best season: *All year - but not advisable on wet and windy days due to the exposed ridge at section 3.*

John Watson

SCARLET BANKSIA

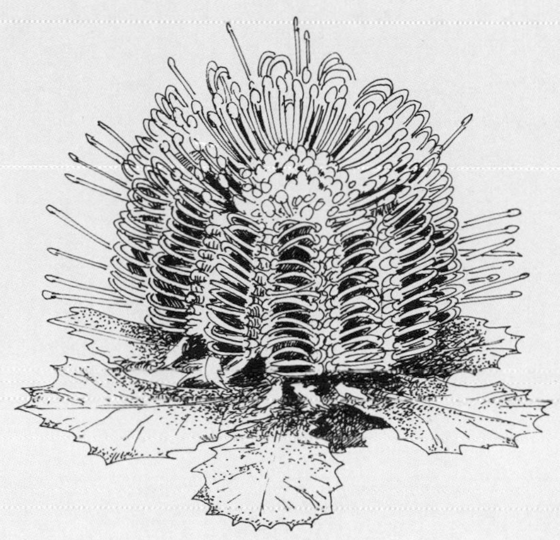

Scarlet banksia *(Banksia coccinea)* is one of WA's most well-known banksias, despite being confined to a relatively small area. Scarlet banksia is found from west of Albany and the Stirling Range to the Young River. It grows on sandy or gravelly soils in heath, shrubland or woodland. It is one of few red banksias, as most species have yellow, orange or brown flower-spikes. The vivid flower heads take their colour from the scarlet styles of the numerous soft, furry flowers.

The plant is used extensively as a long-lasting cut flower. However, because pickers can spread disease, such as dieback and canker, wild populations may not be harvested. Like many banksias, scarlet banksia is easily killed by fire and threatened by the introduced dieback fungus (*Phytophthora cinnamomi*).

Scarlet banksia grows up to four metres or more. The rigid, leathery leaves are blunt at the tip and have prickly teeth. The flower heads appear from May to January. They are six to 12 centimetres long and just as wide, with many closely-packed flowers. Individual flowers are greyish-white and about three centimetres long, but have protruding scarlet styles, which are initially curved then straighten out. Woody fruits, only six to eight millimetres across and hairy, form in the squat cones. They release their seeds after fire.

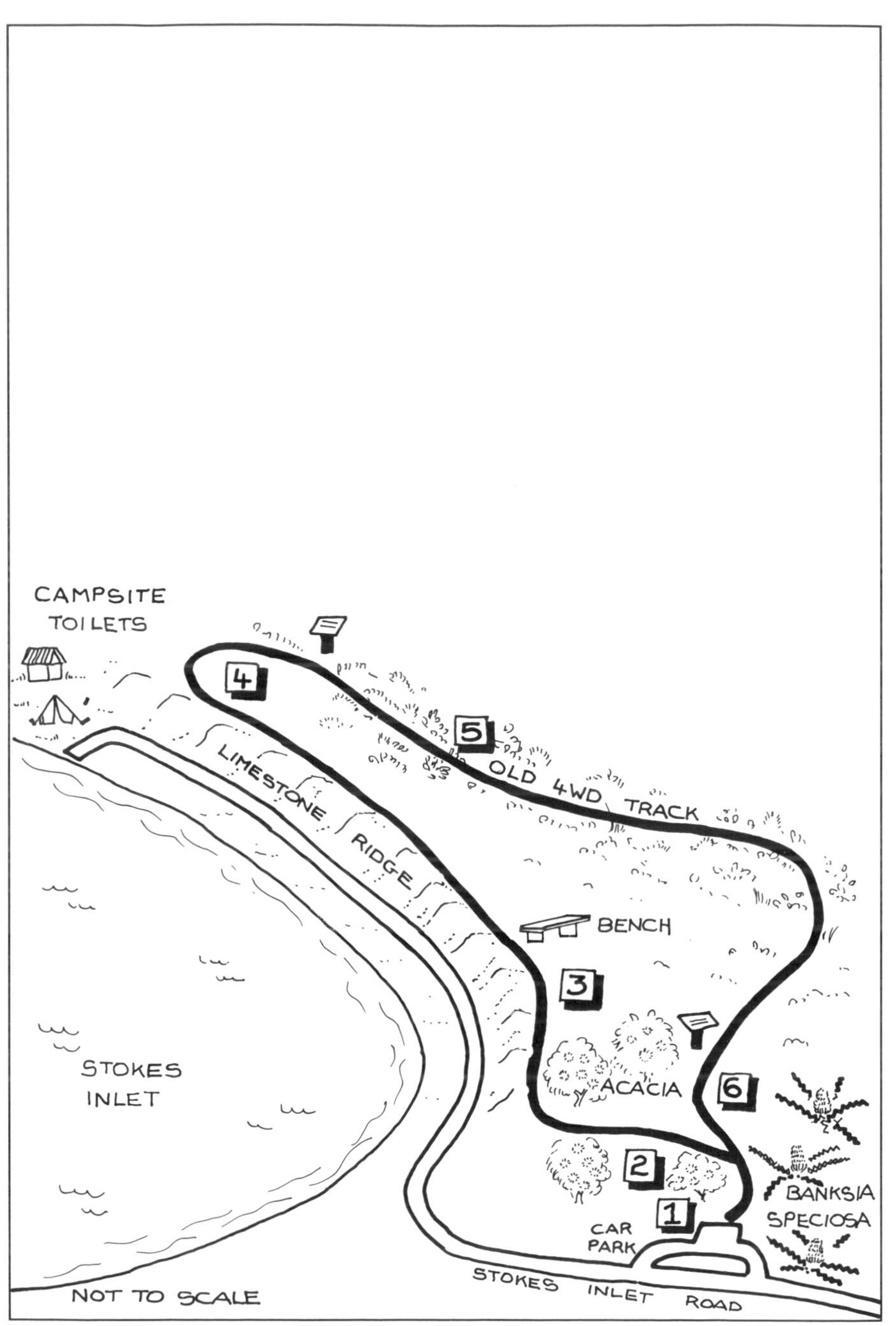
CAMPSITE
TOILETS
4
5
OLD 4WD TRACK
LIMESTONE
RIDGE
BENCH
3
ACACIA
6
2
1
CAR
PARK
BANKSIA
SPECIOSA
STOKES
INLET
STOKES INLET ROAD
NOT TO SCALE

Stokes Heritage Trail

47

Stokes National Park

Length: *1.8 km circuit.*
Grade: *1 (but some uneven and loose sections over limestone rock).*
Walk time: *40 minutes.*

This path is part of the Western Australian Heritage Trails Network established in 1988 as a Bicentennial Commemorative Program. It provides excellent views across Stokes Inlet and is interpreted by plaques along the way.

1. The heritage trail begins at the car park about 600 metres before the southern terminus of Stokes Inlet Road. An introduction to the trail is provided on a large interpretive panel at this point.
2. Follow the gravel path for about 20 metres to where it forks and take the left branch. After another 100 metres, the gravel finishes and the path begins to climb through red-eyed wattle (*Acacia cyclops*) to the start of the limestone ridge.
3. After about 80 metres of steady ascent the first lookout point across the inlet is reached. A bit further on there is a bench on which to sit and reflect.
4. After several hundred metres along the edge of the cliff, the path turns sharply right for 30 metres then right again along an old overgrown four-wheel-drive track.
5. Follow the track back to the base of the limestone escarpment, passing through vegetation of frog hakea (*Hakea nitida*), cockies tongues (*Templetonia retusa*), ridge-fruited mallee (*Eucalyptus angulosa*) and white clematis (*Clematis pubescens*).
6. Rejoin a gravel path which soon leads back to the fork at point 2. There are fine specimens of showy banksia (*Banksia speciosa*) in this vicinity. This species extends from Hopetoun to the Israelite Bay area. It usually flowers all year.

Where is it? *80 km west of Esperance via South Coast Highway and Stokes Inlet Road.*
Travelling time: *1 hour from Esperance.*
Facilities: *Toilets at terminus campsite 600 m along Stokes Inlet Road.*
On-site information: *Interpretive plaques; some track markers along the way.*
Best season: *All year - an easy walk which gives a great introduction to the natural and cultural history of Stokes National Park.*

John Watson

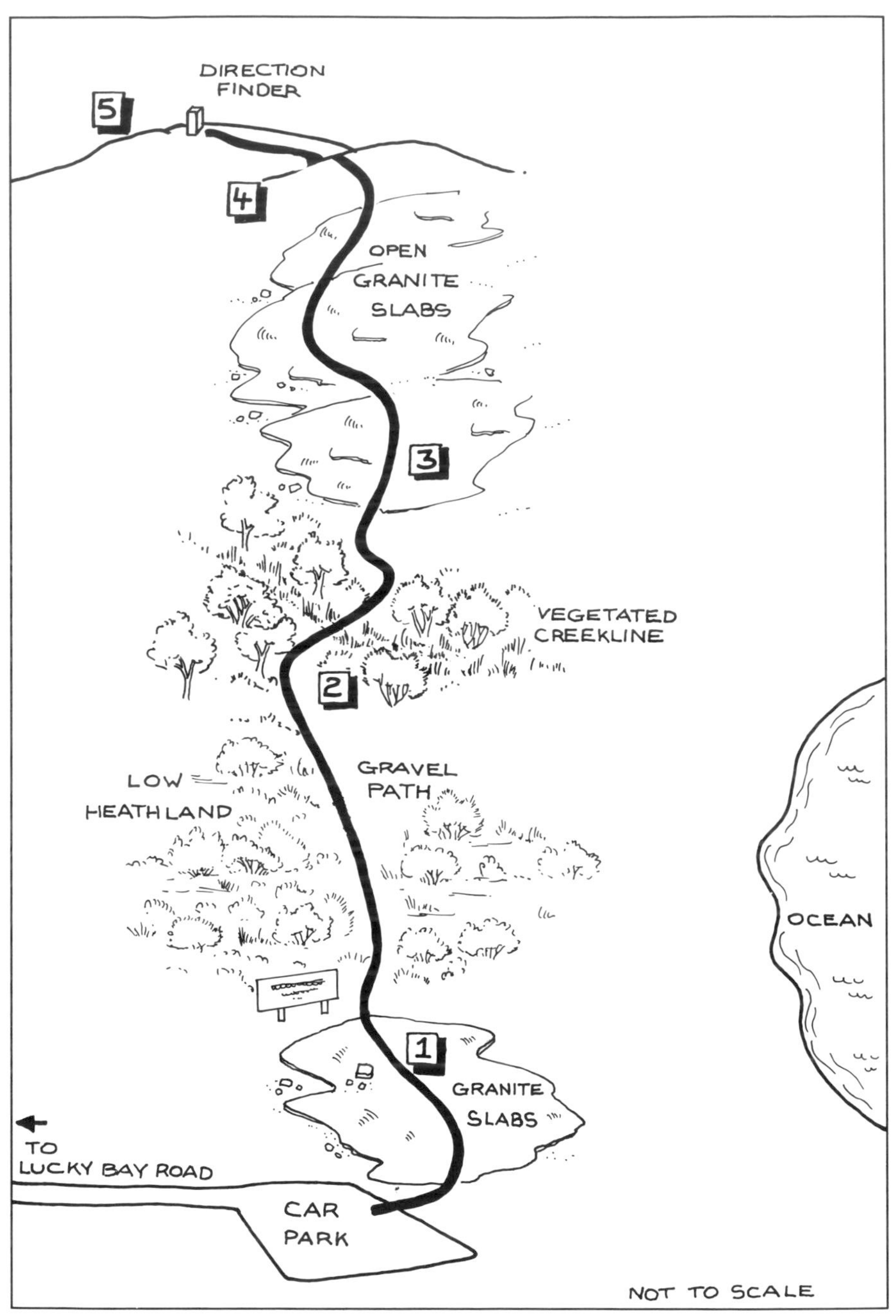
DIRECTION
FINDER
5
4
OPEN
GRANITE
SLABS
3
VEGETATED
CREEKLINE
2
GRAVEL
PATH
LOW
HEATHLAND
OCEAN
1
GRANITE
SLABS
TO
LUCKY BAY ROAD
CAR
PARK
NOT TO SCALE

Cape Le Grand Heritage Trail 48

Cape Le Grand National Park

Length: *1.5 km return.*
Grade: *1.*
Walk time: *40 minutes.*

This path is part of the Coastal Trail between Le Grand Beach and Rossiter Bay. It is also part of the South Coast Heritage Trails Network. Instead of returning to your start point you can continue to Lucky Bay and then return by the same route or, alternatively, arrange a lift back to Thistle Cove.

1. From the Thistle Cove car park follow the signs towards Lucky Bay, initially crossing a flat granite slab to reach the heritage trail sign.
2. Follow the gravel path across low heathlands for about 300 metres, when the path heads right into some taller vegetation.
3. There is often a stream flowing in this vicinity and frogs are usually heard calling. After about 30 metres, you emerge onto more open granite slabs which rise gradually for several hundred metres to the top of the hill. The correct route is marked by rock cairns with marker posts.
4. At the top of the hill you can glimpse Rossiter Bay to the east. Descend a short distance and then up onto the final rocky ridge, where a direction finder is located on a stone plinth. This plaque points out the direction and distance to several historic locations including Rossiter Bay, Thistle Cove, Mississippi Hill, Frenchman Peak, Mount Le Grand. These locations are named after the following early explorers or visitors: Citizen Le Grand, who arrived with the D'Entrecasteaux expedition in 1792; Mr Thistle, who was with the Flinders expedition in 1802; and Mr Rossiter, who was Captain of the whaler *Mississippi* in 1841.
5. You may continue east along the Coastal Trail to Lucky Bay (also named by Flinders), about 20 minutes easy walking. Alternatively, you could retrace your steps to Thistle Cove.

Where is it? *60 km east of Esperance via Merivale Road, Cape Le Grand Road and Lucky Bay Road.*
Travelling time: *1 hour from Esperance.*
Facilities: *Picnic table. Camping and toilet facilities at Lucky Bay.*
Best season: *All year.*

Klaus Tiedemann

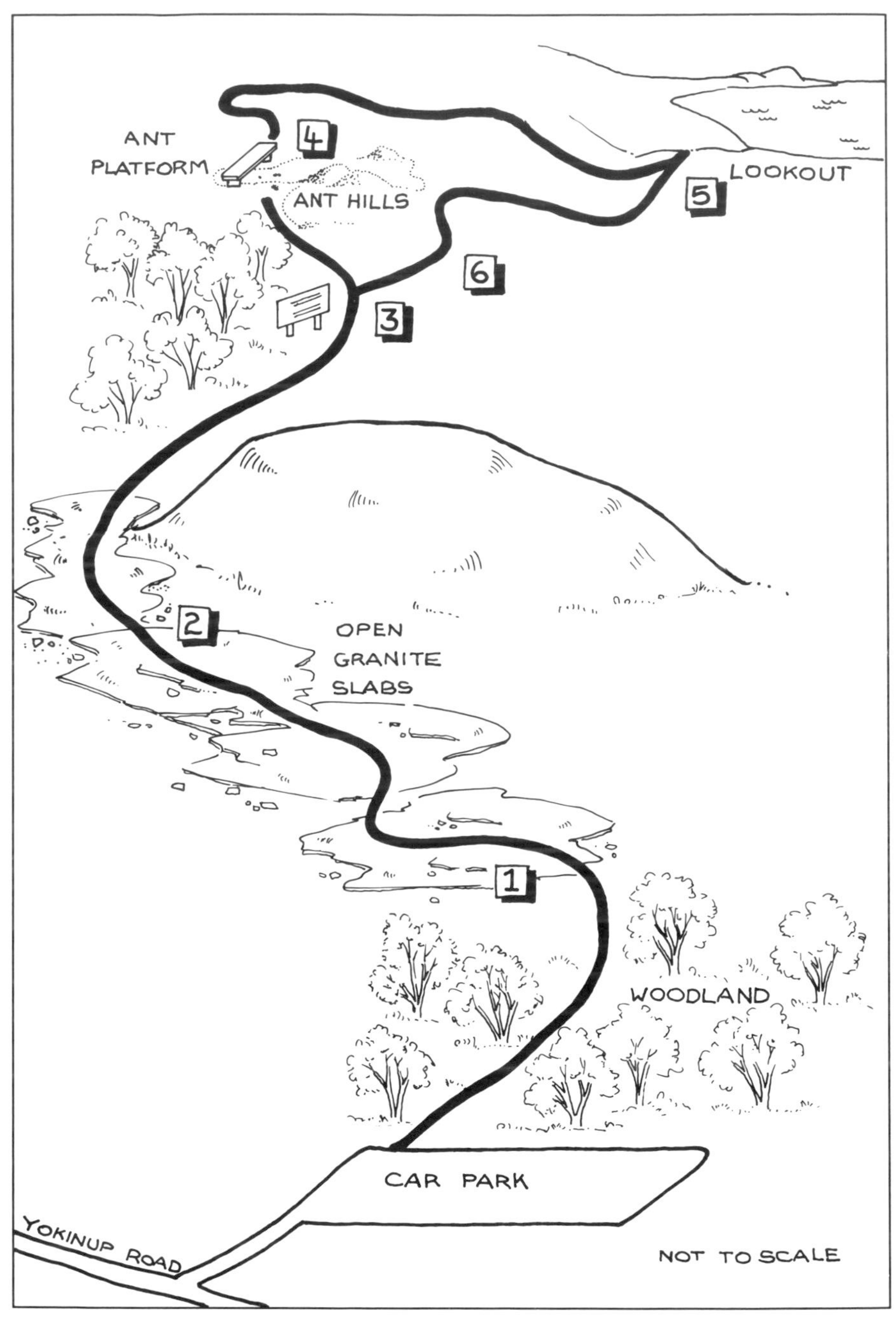
ANT PLATFORM
4
ANT HILLS
LOOKOUT
5
6
3
2
OPEN GRANITE SLABS
1
WOODLAND
CAR PARK
YOKINUP ROAD
NOT TO SCALE

Len Otte Nature Trail

49

Belinup Hill, Cape Arid National Park

Length: *2 km.*
Grade: *1.*
Walk time: *1 hour.*

Do not wear open shoes. Ants are numerous along the trail, especially around steps 2 - 4. Use the viewing platform provided or keep moving!

This nature trail was established in 1979 by Len Otte, the first resident ranger at Cape Arid National Park. Len was a dedicated ranger who passed away unexpectedly whilst on duty in July 1981. The trail has been dedicated as a fitting memorial of Len's achievements and life at Cape Arid National Park. This nature trail was the first to be established in a WA national park. The route followed and the on-site descriptions are still very much as presented in 1979.

1. On leaving the car park, pass through a short section of yate (*Eucalyptus occidentalis*) woodland for about 300 metres, then swing left and emerge onto an area of open granite slabs
2. Follow the markers, veering slightly right at first and then round the left side of the large dome, to arrive at the top of the hill after about 400 metres.
3. A short distance into the woodland on your left you will reach the trailhead sign, which marks the commencement of the interpretive section of the nature trail. A few metres further on, take the left fork of the track and follow the markers and numbered wooden pegs. See the on-site information for details of each numbered stopping point.
4. You reach an 'ant viewing' platform. Even in mid-winter the ants can be very active so do use the platform and take care to wear footwear that covers your feet!
5. A lookout is a great place to soak up the history and atmosphere of Cape Arid. From this point, you can see Mount Ragged some 60 km to the north-east, Mount Arid to the south-east and Middle Island to the south-south-east. Thomas River, and the sweeping area arc of Yokinup Bay, lies in the foreground.
6. Continue along the trail until you rejoin the circuit and turn left to pass the trailhead sign once more. Return to the car park along the outward route.

Where is it? *140 km from Esperance via Fisheries Road, Tagon Road, Yokinup Road.*

Travelling time: *1½ hours.*
Facilities*: Full camping facilities including toilets at campsite a few hundred metres on towards the beach.*
On-site information: *Path markers, numbered pegs and interpretive brochure and/or plaques.*
Best season*: All year, but beware of ant activity in summer!*

John Watson

Index by Walk Lengths

Length (return)	Name	Region	Walk no.
4 km	Canal Rocks to Wyadup	Limestone Coast	14
4 km	Brook and Bridge Walk	Limestone Coast	16
4 km	Big Brook Dam	Karri Forest	20
4 km	Toolbrunup Peak	Mountains and Sea Cliffs	38
4 km	Castle Rock	Mountains and Sea Cliffs	40
4 km	Point Possession Heritage Trail	Mountains and Sea Cliffs	41
4.5 km	Heathlands Walk	Limestone Coast	8
5 km	Boorara Tree	Karri Forest	24
5 km	Bluff Knoll	Mountains and Sea Cliffs	37
5.5 km	The Rocks Walktrail	Karri Forest	25
5.5 km	Nancy Peak	Mountains and Sea Cliffs	39
6 km	Lake Pollard	Limestone Coast	7
6 km	Coalmine Beach	Karri Forest	30
6.5 km	Hamelin Bay to Cosy Corner	Limestone Coast	17
8 km	Harris Dam	Jarrah Forest	2
8 km	Great Forest Trees Walk	Karri Forest	26
8 km	Mount Lindesay	Karri Forest	35
9.4 km	Sika Circuit	Jarrah Forest	3
14 km	Maxwell Trail	Jarrah Forest	6
15 km	Greenbushes Loop	Jarrah Forest	4

CALM Offices

METROPOLITAN

WA Naturally Information Centre
47 Henry Street
FREMANTLE
☎ (08) 9430 8600
Open: 10 am to 5.30 pm every day except Tuesday

State Operations Headquarters
50 Hayman Road
COMO 6152
☎ (08) 9334 0333 Fax (08) 9334 0466.

SWAN REGION

Regional Office
3044 Albany Highway
KELMSCOTT 6000
☎ (08) 9390 5977 Fax (08) 9390 7059

District Office
Banksiadale Road
DWELLINGUP 6213
☎ (08) 9538 1078 Fax (08) 9538 1203

CENTRAL FOREST REGION

Regional Office
North Boyanup Road
BUNBURY
☎ (08) 9725 4300 Fax (08) 9725 4351

District Offices
147 Wittenoom Street
COLLIE 6225
☎ (08) 9734 1988 Fax (08) 9734 4539

CENTRAL FOREST REGION

District Offices (cont.)
14 Queen Street
BUSSELTON 6280
☎ (08) 9752 1677 Fax (08) 9752 1432

South Western Highway
KIRUP 6261
☎ (08) 9731 6232

SOUTHERN FOREST REGION

Regional Office
Brain Street
MANJIMUP 6258
☎ (08) 9771 7948 Fax (08) 9777 1363

District Offices
Kennedy Street
PEMBERTON
☎ (08) 9776 1207 Fax (08) 9776 1410

South Western Highway
WALPOLE 6398
☎ (08) 9840 1027 Fax (08) 9840 1251

SOUTH COAST REGION

Regional Office
120 Albany Highway
ALBANY 6330
☎ (08) 9842 4500 Fax (08) 9841 3329

District Office
92 Dempster Street
ESPERANCE 6450
☎ (08) 9071 3733 Fax (08) 9071 3657

Notes

Notes

4327-1097-12500